The Paralysis of International Institutions and the Remedies

The Paralysis of International Institutions and the Remedies

A Study of Self-Determination, Concord among the Major Powers, and Political Arbitration

István Bibó
*Formerly Professor
of the University of Szeged*

With an Introduction by
Professor Bernard Crick

A Halsted Press Book

John Wiley & Sons
New York

Published in the U.S.A. by
The Halsted Press, a Division of
John Wiley & Sons, Inc. New York

Computer typeset by Input Typesetting, London
and printed in Great Britain by
Redwood Burn Limited, Trowbridge & Esher

Library of Congress Cataloging in Publication Data

Bibó, István.
    The paralysis of international institutions and the
remedies.

    "A Halsted Press book."
        1. Self-determination, National.   2. Pacific settle-
ment of international disputes.   3. Arbitration, International.   4. International organization.   I. Title.
JX4054.B47   1976   341.26   75-17182
ISBN 0-470-07208-3

Contents

Contents

Author's Preface

For a variety of reasons, it has not been possible for me to amplify this work as fully as is customary in a serious study, nor to provide the usual full bibliographical notes. Yet I feel I must give an account of the chief outside stimuli which contributed so much towards the conception of the present text. First and foremost is the teaching of that master of Hungarian legal philosophy, Berna Horvath, on the role that the concepts of power, conflict and procedure have to play in the spheres of law, state and the international community, as well as on the justifying and revolutionising functions of common law. A further strong impulse was provided by the generally underestimated thoughts of Guglielmo Ferrero on the proper interpretation of the principle of legitimacy: these he documented in a particularly striking way through his presentation of the basic principles and functioning of the European monarchic system between the seventeenth century and the First World War. On the question as to whether power may be made humane, I benefited from contrasting the rather sceptical views of Bertrand Russell and Raymond Aron with those of Robert M. MacIver, the latter being more optimistic and, for me at any rate, more convincing. In analysing the concepts of nation and nationalism, I fully concurred with Dankwart A. Rustow and Hugh Seton-Watson in that it is impossible to equate the nation, as a communal fact and form of consciousness, with nationalism as an almost always harmful ideology of domination; thus the analysis and interpretation of the phenomena of the nation must not be confused with a rejection of nationalism.

I thought, therefore, that the distinction made by Jan Huizinga and the classic authors of Marxism — starting from very different ideological and theoretical premises but not differing widely so far as moral and social tone are concerned — between patriotism and nationalism is significant, useful and worthy of further elaboration. I benefited greatly from Raymond Aron's work on *Peace and War*. I read with great attention but much doubt Arnold Toynbee's train of thought, recently published, on the past and future possibilities of groping towards a world state. On the question of the ultimate bases of the international community, I think the debate between Hans Kelsen and Alfred Verdross thirty years ago is still instructive: in this connection I found Kelsen's contentions significant, chiefly in that they aroused my spirit of contradiction. Similarly, I have been remembering these past thirty years some poignant remarks on the nature of international jurisdiction made by Paul Guggenheim. Also useful has been the basic work by Leland Goodrich and Edward Hambro on the Charter of the United Nations: the comprehensive book on the same subject written by Hans Kelsen; Leon Gordenker's work on the function of the U.N. Secretary General; Laszlo Puza's writing (in Hungarian) on the new international law; and Rolin Farquharson's book on the theory of referenda. I had hoped to add case studies of the Cyprus dispute and of the Arab-Israeli conflict, but space has not allowed. Finally, I must thank all those who have helped me in translating and editing my manuscript.

ISTVAN BIBO
Spring, 1975

INTRODUCTION

Bernard Crick

Professor of Politics, Birkbeck College, the University of London;
Joint Editor of *The Political Quarterly*

When three years ago two chapters of this book and a table of contents were shown to me, I immediately saw, despite what was then merely a quick and literal translation, that this was a work of real importance, and I was determined that it should be properly published. Now, thanks to the care and patience of, several good friends, a proper translation has been made. I write this introduction simply to put the book in context and to say something about the author, who has not previously been translated into English, though his earlier works made him famous on the continent of Europe.

After reading it all, I have become convinced that this book is worthy to be numbered among those very few which have addressed themselves to what is still humanity's greatest problem — how to preserve peace in a way that can be accepted as just. Such books are likely to be remembered. From out of one of the most troubled but civilised countries of Europe, Hungary, comes a quiet and unspectacular, yet courageous and scholarly, humanistic but practical voice which argues against both the false idealism of 'world government' and the false realism of 'since not world government then simply the self-interest of the Great Powers'. Istvan Bibo, who has held high office but now lives very quietly, argues against false idealism by showing clearly that we can but — and mostly love to — live in nations, but that national feeling and nationalism are to be sharply distinguished; and he argues against false realism by showing that in fact there have been fairly clear principles in the conduct of international relations, certainly before 1914, and that these could be extended to fit the needs both of a democratic age and of a time of ideological confrontation.

He states a case, based on a wide and deep reading of European history, for thinking that international political arbitration could be nearer than we think. He builds from what we have known: the principle of national self-determination — which with all its difficulties has been a great liberating factor – and types of concord between great powers. The Concert of Powers and the rules of diplomacy that followed the Congress of Vienna are bad examples of these in their content, indeed, but not, he dares to remind us, in method. Working from these and working within these limits could yet lead to new institutions of arbitration.

This is a book which deserves to be studied carefully in every country of the world. And however it is now received, I am convinced that it will be looked back to as the beginning of a time of, as it were, a realistic idealism; it is a cool, rather dry and at times even a fussily academic demonstration, but a convincing demonstration that there is no need to fear that international peace can never find strong institutions, must always depend upon accidents of temporary great power accord; but that we can slowly but surely abolish war, achieve Immanuel Kant's reasoned vision of perpetual peace. The book was mainly written two or three years ago. References to Kissinger's diplomacy are not to be found in it. But I feel sure that that other careful student of Metternich would not wish to deny that even the most energetic, subtle and realistic great power diplomacy needs to work through new institutions – if every quarrel between lesser powers means either war or a crisis involving the great powers. Mr Kissinger might be the first to admit that peace cannot depend upon the continued existence of other people like himself. Nothing is likely to date the major part of Istvan Bibo's argument.

It may help to understand the viewpoint of the book better if I relate what I have learned about the author from friends of his in England. Istvan Bibo was born in 1911. He belongs therefore to the generation which in childhood experienced the upheavals of the First World War, the overthrow of the Austro-Hungarian monarchy, the Hungarian Revolution in its two stages – the republican, democratic government of Count Karolyi, and then Béla Kun's famous but short-lived Soviet-style republic; then the counter-revolution which brought Admiral Horthy to power and the breaking up of the historical territory of Hungary by the Trianon Treaty. When the depression of 1929 struck Hungary, Bibo had just become a student of the Faculty of Law at Szeged University. He continued his studies in Geneva, becoming a Ph.D. in Political Science. He obtained a position as a magistrate in Hungary and, while carrying out his official work, broadened the scope of his knowledge, in particular of history. His studies strengthened his opposition to the official views of contemporary history.

In a Hungary which had been defeated and dismembered, the 'revisionist' ideology of revenge, heavily tinged with racism towards the peoples of the neighbouring countries, was dominant. If only in reaction to Allied Powers, the influence of Germany spread. Academic historians began to picture Hungary as part of a Germano-Catholic civilisation. Bibo, however, belonged to another school whose origins were deeply rooted in Hungarian political thought. He followed those 'politique' statesmen of the sixteenth and seventeenth centuries who, thanks to a policy of realism, managed to maintain a practically independent national Hungarian nucleus in Transylvania – those who took the best advantage of the tragic position of a Hungary caught between the Austrian anvil and the Turkish hammer.

Bibo therefore belonged to the 'populist' movement which instigated a whole series of enquiries into rural life, the so-called 'sociographical' research which endeavoured, both in novels and monographs, to get a greater understanding of peasant populations and to narrow the gap between the intellectual élite of the towns and the peasants. His friend Gyula Illyès' documentary novel, *The People of the Puszta,* is only the more internationally famous of this literature. On the political level, the 'populist' movement was opposed to a revisionist nationalism and to fascism, which was rapidly progressing in Hungary on the eve of the Second World War. They favoured agrarian reform, the great hope of three million landless peasants, but were opposed to great experiments of collectivisation on the Kolkoz model. The Fascist threat for a time threw them politically closer, both to the Socialist left-wing and to the Communists, but they kept their original ideology which was far removed from Marxism.

Bibo's public life began under the anti-Fascist coalition that was set up by the conquering allies in 1945. This was a coalition of four parties: the Communists, the Social Democrats, the National Peasants and the Smallholders. The Minister of the Interior, member of the National Peasants' Party (which was the political form of the Populist movement), put him in charge of the Department of Public Administration. The policy of the coalition went back to the 'March Front', a resistance movement created in the middle of the war by populist intellectuals. Bibo was heavily involved in the policies of the coalition. The Communist Party at first worked with the other parties in a mutually tolerant manner, but when the first general elections gave an absolute majority to the Smallholders' Party, the most right-wing party of the coalition, a clash with the Communist Party and the occupying power became inevitable.

In this crisis Bibo wrote and published, not without difficulty, a notable article called 'The Crisis of Hungarian Democracy'. He tried to define and defend a creative middle position between any threat of restoration of the *ancien régime* and the alleged need of a dictatorship of the proletariat. He called himself neither liberal nor socialist, but a passionate believer in both freedom and social reform, but social reform based on an empirical examination of national conditions, not on the copying of foreign examples – whether of East or West.

In 1946 he drew up the text of a Constitutional Bill of Rights (which, needless to say, was not adopted), and in the spring of that year he wrote a pamphlet called *The Misery of the Small Countries of Eastern Europe*. In 1947 he wrote an article on the character of the police repression of the ever-growing number of 'plots'. In 1948 it became impossible to publish any more warnings or attacks. His last essay in that year before a long silence was an historical examination of the Jewish question in Hungary, but its topical points were clear: that rabid nationalism in the past had so corrupted authentic national feeling, which respects the freedom of others, that now many Hungarian intellectuals were inhibited by guilt from offering a bold resistance to the Stalinist dictatorship of Rakosi, which professed to destroy all the evils of the past, and much else besides.

He lost his official posts, and although for a short while he was named Professor of Political Science at Szeged University, he was quickly dismissed from this post and was not allowed to return to Budapest until Imre Nagy's first government in 1953-4, and only then as a minor employee of the university library.

Very late in the uprising of 1956, Imrey Nagy, Chairman of the Council of Ministers, formed the new coalition government and made Bibo a Minister of State — having been elected as a member of the executive committee of the newly reconstituted National-Peasant Party. Very late indeed — on 3 November 1956. On the morning of 4 November he stayed typing in his office in the national parliament while Soviet troops occupied the building. They must have thought he was some minor clerk carrying on with his work irrespective of regime. In fact he was writing what became a famous proclamation, part of which said:

> 'Hungary has no intention of carrying out an anti-Soviet policy; on the contrary, she intends to take her proper place in the community of the free people of Eastern Europe who wish to live their lives under the aegis of freedom, justice and of a society freed of exploitation . . .
>
> To suggest that it was necessary to bring an enormous foreign army into the country is cynical and ridiculous. It is the very presence of this army which is the main source of disquiet and trouble . . .
>
> The Hungarian people has paid ample tribute of its blood to show the world its attachment to freedom and justice. It is now the turn of the world powers to show the strength of the principles expressed in the United Nations Charter, the strength of the freedom-loving peoples. I ask the great powers and the United Nations to make wise and courageous decisions for the liberty of the enslaved nations . . .'

Having signed this, as Minister of State, he had copies duplicated, then calmly walked out of the building through the troops surrounding it, and had the copies distributed, by one means or another. By 9 November he had finished a small pamphlet, *Proposal for a Compromise Solution of the Hungarian Problem*, which was distributed in the same way. Many felt that he was the last courageous moderate voice to speak for the Hungarian nation, especially when he wrote another document, *Hungary and the World Situation,* which was informally distributed inside Hungary and published abroad in 1957.

This last document could be seen as the seeds of this book. For he tried to show that states such as Hungary, militarily weak and ideologically torn, are test cases for whether the great powers can coexist with both internal and external stability. Third World countries must see themselves, he argued, as being similarly forced into choices of allegiance they do not want and which would perpetuate, not solve, problems. It had to be demonstrated to them that countries like Hungary could enjoy substantial freedom within the Soviet bloc — just as it would be realistic for Soviet diplomacy not to try to gain the allegiance of South American states, but to gain for them a substantial degree of independence from the United States.

He was imprisoned on 27 May 1957 and tried *in camera* in September 1958, being sentenced to life imprisonment. He was, however, released from prison in 19?? and has lived quietly ever since, thinking, reading, writing: a great and internationally famous Hungarian intellectual and patriot. The essays I refer to I have read — for they were translated in London around 1959 and prepared for publication by a man now dead, whose biographical notes on Bibo I have drawn on freely. But the essays were not published, it being felt that their publication might have prejudiced any chance of his release in milder times. Happily the cautiousness proved justified, he was released. Happily the times now do seem to be just that much milder amid the spirit of *detente.*

The argument of the book

There are no topical political references in the book, certainly not to Hungarian politics and the events of 1956. The book is deliberately and intellectually, not out of prudence, written at a high level of generality. The argument can be applied to any situation of conflict. The author is well aware, as a widely read and cosmopolitan mind (in the best sense of that abused term) despite his somewhat restricted opportunities for travel or contact with foreign scholars of late, that East Europeans have an international reputation for being a bit obsessional about their troubles — as well they may. This elephant belongs to the world, however, not to the Polish or Hungarian question. If from time to time he draws on his own national history, it is only because Hungary, like other small Central and Eastern European countries, furnishes a ready and relevant example of the acute problems of what he calls, probably from the German, 'state-formation'. Africa and South-east Asia know these problems too.

'State-formation' is a phrase that recurs often. If it sounds odd to English ears, it is perhaps because I say 'English' and not, more sensibly, 'British'. We too are discovering, after the end of Empire, problems of 'state-formation'. Is there really a British state, or is it an English state imposed on Scotland, Wales and Northern Ireland? This is beginning to be a serious question. And it is not the same concept as national self-determination, for it raises the juridical questions of what are to be the boundaries and the powers of the new states. No state whatever is now fully sovereign; not even the U.S.S.R., the U.S.A. or China can control their internal affairs fully independently of the outside world; but no state would regard its political institutions as genuinely national if they were only on sufferance from the enabling power, or if they only had some shadow-power of an attenuated federalism. So 'state-formation' it is. There is no point in translating away into a series of elegant synonyms a concept which properly lumps together things of which our very language shows how little experience we have had, or that we have tried deliberately to keep apart — now with less success than in the past. As if, for example, the problem of Northern Ireland was something utterly unique and exceptional — East and Central Europeans must smile at us for this myopic belief.

The original manuscript did contain two long and detailed sections showing how Bibo's argument could be applied to two difficult concrete cases: Cyprus and the Arab-Israeli conflict. The specific nature of these have, however, dated them somewhat and they would have made this book a forbidding length, so as editor I have taken the responsibility of not publishing them, at least for the moment, but simply of putting copies in the Library of the Royal Institute of International Affairs, London, of the British Museum, the Library of Congress and the New York Public Library. They may be copied but not published. They were appendices to the general argument, which is all translated.

Bibo's historical starting point is the seeming paralysis of international institutions: the weakness of the U.N., the clear will to achieve peace between the great powers, but the lack of permanent institutions and shared principles to make this seem assured (or rather, lack of a clear perception that they do share some principles already), so that each national conflict could be less than a world crisis seeming to call for extraordinary measures, 'crisis diplomacy'. His theoretical starting point is what I would call an humanistic realism: 'self-interest and military power cannot manage without moral and idealistic justifications, nor can ideals and institutions function without an element of self-interest and power'. He exposes the illusion of the so-called purely practical man that he is, in fact, purely practical, rather than working by some dimly perceived and often outmoded doctrine; and of the idealist, that all would be well by wishing it well — or the grim converse, that since nothing ever is judged in those terms, then no holds are barred.

If these sentiments seem banalities, he makes them come to life. He shows, first, what in fact were the agreements on principle that existed between the nineteenth-century concert of powers. He shows their limitations, certainly: but the main point is not the outdated or even, at the time, repressive content of them; but that they existed. As did a new set of principles when national self-determination became both the doctrine of internal politics and the theory of international relations.

In Chapter 6 he shows the weaknesses of national self-determination as the sole principle of international order. But he does not pose a false antithesis between international anarchy and an international government; rather, he sets out to show the conditions in which national sentiment can underpin the ability of governments to work towards new international institutions. The internal links are vital. Different kinds of democracy exist, and should exist. But everywhere in the twentieth century the dependence of governments on their populations, if they are to exercise real power – towards both peace and welfare – is greater than ever before. Diplomacy can no longer be simply a matter of élites. Other leaders need to know that other leaders will, in fact, be followed, able to honour agreements – particularly those concerned with boundaries, minorities and state-formation.

> 'Experience shows that a strong link between those in power and the common will is essential, and it is dangerous for a government to feel itself able and entitled to lead the passive, ignorant masses on the road to happiness without their consent. There are frightening examples that show how the most competent, sincere and incorruptible government and élite can, in a surprisingly short time, become senselessly tyrannical, cynically disillusioned and shamelessly corrupt.'

The author shows how such a seemingly old-fashioned and discredited juridical concept as 'the sovereignty of the people' must form the basis of legitimacy, however much the forms may vary, in any state which is stable, and how any state whose governments are perpetually unstable, automatically presents continual threats to international order. In a way, the book presents a philosophical and juridical justification of the change in world politics of the last twenty years from concern with ideological victory to concern with stability. But Bibo marshals all the oldest arguments of political science and prudence – which are true – to show that imposed stabilities are, in fact, rarely likely to last, are always potentially explosive as when ... and every reader will supply his own examples; far better that the author has not.

He is, in fact, more concrete by not getting bogged down in particular cases. How concrete he is can be seen, for instance, in Chapter 9: 'The Inadequacy of Present-Day Methods for Settling Political Disputes' – which I think is the keystone of the book. He reduces the practice of the old nineteenth-century diplomacy to eight propositions or generalisations, some of them almost comically specific, but clearly true – such as '(i) There were a few, uncomplicated and expedient formalities that were taken seriously and with mutual courtesy . . . (iv) The parties showed a regard for their respective strengths, without constantly and rudely drawing attention to this.' Indeed the chapter begins by identifying with masterly insight and clarity some thirteen contrasts between the new system and the old – though never once does he suggest putting the clock back; rather, radically forward. And he characterises in realistic terms and in seven generalisations the present spirit and technique of international relations, beginning:

> '(i) Formalities have become hollow or uncertain, combining empty and stiff politeness with impulsive or deliberate rudeness and sarcasm. There is constant risk that the entire negotiation will founder in childish squabbles over procedure or prestige – such as the question of the shape of the conference table. This puts the technique of international negotiations back to the stage it had reached in the seventeenth century.'

Yet we have, he argues, however surprisingly, avoided total disaster. His keen realism spends little time indeed on the old nuclear war fears. Nuclear or not, any further total war, such as in the two World Wars, would now prove fatal to civilisation. We have survived because, as I read his argument, of four factors: mutual fear; the survival among the great powers of some of the principles and conventions which governed the old diplomacy; that public opinion now severely limits, most often, rather than enhances the bellicosity of governments; and because some of the institutions of the U.N. represent, in however tangled and difficult a form, the reality of arbitration. In the last two chapters he tries to show how we could move forward from these three points to re-establish, or rather to establish, new principles and conventions governing international order and to create political machinery for settling political disputes.

Istvan Bibo's scholarship comes out of a juridical tradition of writing about politics (which has set the translators some problems), very different from the empirically oriented Anglo-American tradition or the philosophical and ideological tradition in Germany and Russia. But his own originality lies in his intense political realism. He does not enter into rights and wrongs of the disputes themselves, not because he is afraid to or because he dwells amid abstract legalistic concepts; on the contrary, but because, like a wise family lawyer, he knows it is vain to try to reason either side out of 'their rights', but that it is possible with knowledge, patience and skill to suggest procedures by which each may maintain their integrity without damaging the other and, of course, themselves. The disputants may have to moderate some of their behaviour, if they are not to tear down the only house that humanity has, but he shows that we need not expect them to change their behaviour utterly. That is too much to ask. Besides, why should they? To find what we have in common and need in common is not to abolish real and proper differences.

As in Hobbes' *Leviathan,* Bibo ends this small masterpiece of practical reason with a short summary and conclusion. Some may choose to read it first. But the grounds of the argument, so clearly and shrewdly set out, are what will convince.

[1]

The Paralysis of the International Community in Settling International Disputes

The increasing number of unsettled international disputes

The fact that we have been unable since the Second World War to settle the really critical disputes of international relations stems from the lack of principles and ideas in this crucial area. This is especially true in the attempts to reach permanent settlements of territorial disputes and conflicts arising from the formation of new states. The number of unresolved situations, which languish in a more or less static condition, has increased alarmingly. Cease-fire lines and truce demarcation lines take the place of final national boundaries; states are arbitrarily and illogically brought into being as temporary solutions to particular and pressing problems; and repeated armed clashes between nations and nationalities, with all the inevitable repercussions, seem a permanent part of the contemporary world scene.

All this takes place against a background in which there has been a wholesale degeneration in the tone of international dealings, deadlock in international negotiations, repeated 'incidents', increasing rearmament and local wars which swell the pathetic crowds of refugees. This, together with general uncertainty, affects millions of people all over the world. Also, there are the confrontations between great ideological and military blocs, and more recently the development of the Third World, with all the problems that arise from the different political languages spoken by these groups. If these differences, which threaten the peace of the world, are looked at closely, it seems that they spring not so much from ideological content as from the fact that too often such controversies have become disputes about the formation of states or of their territorial integrity. All of the problems listed are overshadowed by the threat of nuclear war and the possible destruction of mankind. Ironically, it is often precisely this threat that compels the responsible leaders of states and international organisations to give priority to maintaining world peace at any cost. Often this peace is secured by postponing a permanent settlement of an immediate and inflammable problem by unsatisfactory interim solutions.

Much of the recent special diplomacy is of this character.

Another consequence of the nuclear monopoly of the great powers has been the outbreak of a number of 'conventional' wars in diverse places. However, in the changed world scene these wars have not yielded a solution to disputes, as in the past to some extent limited wars did. It is an open question whether the constant increase in the number of unsettled problems, combined with the threat of nuclear war, is not in fact creating a vicious circle. In the circle, fear of nuclear war leads to procrastination over the finding of permanent solutions, whilst conversely the uncertainties born of unsettled crises tend to make nuclear war more likely.

People who, with some justification, see a connection between the political position as stated above and the universal moral, intellectual and social crisis of our time, tend to look for universal answers as they feel a high-level formulation of the problem is called for. This line of reasoning suggests that there should be a *complete* settlement of ideological conflicts either by one side winning or through reconciliations. Nationalism and *nation states* are seen as the nub of most disputes and therefore they should be abolished in favour of *world government, world police,* or *world state.* Theoretically such arguments are very convincing. In reality, however, ideological confrontations are becoming increasingly hostile and are not disappearing, and nationalism, far from losing ground, is more pervasive than ever. If the survival of mankind were really dependent on the polarised ideas described earlier, the situation would be gloomy indeed. But, of course, all fundamental idealistic solutions – unless meant for the cowed survivor of a world catastrophe – necessitate steps being taken to cure actual tensions, danger, uncertainties and unsettled disputes, before any more far-reaching changes can be put into effect.

The inadequacy of current international institutions and procedures for settling international disputes

When looking for possible solutions within the given framework of the international community, we must first discover which fundamentals and generally held principles the community adhere to regarding unsettled problems and disputes. We also need to know what *systems of law* are accepted as valid, and what *procedures, organisations and institutions* are already functioning. An examination of these factors soon reveals that the institutionalised practices of the international community are in the same state of deadlock as are world politics in general.

First, there seems to be some confusion over the fundamental *principles* which could, in theory, be used as generally valid premises for practical application when international disputes arise. To all appearances, the international community does possess some generally accepted and much-respected principles. For instance, it is widely held that the *sovereignty, territorial integrity, and independence* of states must be acknowledged in the interest of peace and stability. Also, that the *people's right to self-determination* must prevail to ensure the correct demarcation of states and to limit abuses of power. These and similar principles are often tied into a nice bouquet and offered like a patent medicine as a cure for the world's ills. However, when it comes to applying these principles to a practical situation, it seems that they are relevant to everything except the specific problem under review. Unfortunately the principles cited are either pure generalities, or are too easily played off one against the other. Some high-minded principle can be found to justify almost any action. After all, most international disputes are not about the validity of the right to sovereignty, territorial integrity, or self-determination but arise over one contestant's claim to territorial integrity against the other's right to self-determination. Alternatively, the dispute may arise over the right of this or that party to claim possession of an area on the principle of territorial integrity. One party may refer to the principle of non-intervention, the other to basic human rights, one to independence and sovereignty, the other to universal interests that overrule these considerations. Despite the fact that sovereignty and the territorial integrity of states are fairly clearly defined in the rules and institutions of international law, it is not easy to determine the contents of and limits to the independence of the state in the midst of the current trend towards international integration. The definition and importance of a people's right to self-determination seems to fluctuate considerably in international law. Although it is customarily referred to in the United Nations Charter and other major documents as a valid or even fundamental principle of international law, many lawyers and politicians deny the existence of this right. They claim it is more harmful than useful. Other factors that are widely cited are nationality, history, ethnic origin, economy, geography, communication and strategy, but no rule or common conviction emerges to clarify the interpolation between these various interests or to confirm their validity.

There can be little doubt that a *system of rules and international law* does in fact exist, despite the confusion over premises and principles. What is far less certain is what the real function of this system can be in respect of the conflicts that affect the order and balance of the community. The functioning of international law is not precisely comparable to that within individual states. Attitudes to international law verge on the schizophrenic. Sometimes its existence alone is expected to deter all states, including the great powers, from committing delinquent acts. More specifically, international law is expected to prevent the onset of wars or the oppression of peoples, and when such events occur international law is then expected to mete out appropriate punishments. When international law is shown to be inadequate to deal with international crises opinion swings to the opposite pole and dismisses it as a giant humbug.

Consequently international law is often ignored and its very real achievements in the long-established fields of valid and effective international treaties and of continuous international arbitration, denied.

Generally, it seems that the set of rules called international law functions smoothly only in those areas which are not deemed of primary importance by the *governing principles of the international community as a whole*. The relegation of international law as a determining agent only in matters of *secondary* importance is most apparent in the *procedures and organisations* which are available for the settlement of political disputes and the solution of repetitive crisis situations. That wars should be averted, that problems, conflicts and crises should be settled peacefully is universally accepted, but what machinery is available for peaceful, international negotiations? Three means are widely accepted: the U.N., *direct negotiation* and internationl *arbitration*. What do these alternatives in fact amount to?

The *U.N. Charter* sets out a fairly flexible procedure of recommendations, proposals, negotiation, mediation, conciliation and even sanctions to be applied if the peace is threatened or broken. However, in the present climate the U.N. is widely and openly regarded as a second-rate forum for world politics. There are at least four reasons why the prestige and standing of the U.N. has declined so dramatically: (a) the great powers can and do ignore the resolutions and rules of the U.N. in matters which directly affect them; (b) habitually the great powers avoid discussing their own vital interests in the U.N.; (c) the high number of valid and binding resolutions passed by the U.N. which have not been obeyed; (d) when the U.N. acts as a tribunal, it has rarely managed to find a permanent solution to the problem in hand.

The shortcomings of the U.N. as a tribunal are well illustrated by the examples of Cyprus and the Arab–Israeli conflicts.

The case of Cyprus was particularly indicative as the U.N. was not only acting as a tribunal but had armed forces on the island to back its decisions. However, as the situation developed it became clear that decisions were being influenced more and more by international factors. Initially the hope was that an international arbitrator backed by an impartial armed force would be able to make judgements based on fundamental principles, but this hope has not been realised. In fact, it seems that the more impartial the forum, the less it refers to philosophic principles.

When the colonial rule of the British in Cyprus was nearing its end, an attempt was made to assess the claims of the Greek and Turkish populations to self-determination. Subsequently a temporary solution was found when a state was formed with a Graeco-Turkish administration under the sponsorship of Greece and Turkey. In the period following the collapse of the joint administration, the Security Council was called in but seems to have achieved little beyond periodically renewing the mandate of the U.N. forces on the island. The Council does not appear to have put forward any clear indication of the purpose or duration of the troops' presence, but limited their role to urging the contestants to make a settlement. This despite the fact that it has always been apparent to any student of the Cyprus situation that a peaceful solution was almost impossible – indeed that was why the U.N. was there. This example leads to the depressing conclusion that the higher the status of the tribunal, the more ineffectual it will be.

The paralysis of the U.N. was even more obvious in the Arab-Israeli conflicts. In all of the three crises in the area before 1973, the U.N. has never managed to achieve more than a very unstable truce or cease-fire agreement. Following the war of 1967, an interim solution evolved which completely ignored the relevant resolutions of the Security Council. The resulting situation was one that all the international agencies, the Great Powers and all interested parties knew could not continue indefinitely and that each day it continued made a new conflagration more inevitable – as occurred. It was inexcusable that the Security Council, most particularly the great powers that sit on it, did not hammer out a limited agreement (at least between themselves) and make a plan of action. While this would have left the problem open-ended, it would at least have put an end to the most absurd aspects of those six wasted years. Even though the balance of power, official attitudes and inflammable local emotions did not hold out much likelihood of a permanent solution, the U.N. showed itself ineffectual at all levels.

Attempts at finding lasting solutions to crises through negotiations between individual countries have not proved effective either. The old conventions of diplomatic interchange and negotiations are now an empty framework and lack even a basic measure of mutual trust and presumptions of good faith. Modern diplomatic negotiations are characterised by an icy politeness that is purely superficial, in which inane formalism alternates with bouts of appalling discourtesy. The parties in contemporary international negotiations do not really negotiate, they merely posture in the roles they imagine will impress the world or, more often, public opinion at home. Discussions are conducted within the rigid limits of declared power politics, unconditional demands, moral admonitions and self-righteousness, and fixed ideological attitudes. Not surprisingly such negotiations tend to be inordinately long, and are rarely successful. When the odd success is achieved it comes mainly from the fortuitous recognition of monetary interests or enforced positions. Because these successes are based on such arbitrary factors, they do not inspire faith in the system from which they emerge. The successes of personal diplomacy by a man like Kissinger are all too likely to prove both personal and temporary. It is very alarming that the phrase 'disputes must be settled through negotiations, not war' sounds empty when the apparently ineffective method of negotiation is the only alternative solution to the apparently effective means of war.

Finally, there is the possibility of peacemaking through international arbitration, though this concept no longer carries the high hopes it inspired in the late nineteenth century. Currently, international arbitration tends to concern itself purely with disputes of a narrowly legal nature which in no way affect vital interests. However, there are still faint calls for a revival of special *international* political arbitration.

Such international order and peace as can be maintained stems not from the satisfactory working of international procedures and institutions, but from (the conclusion is hard to avoid) the balance of power and terror.

The conflict between self-interest and morality in the international community

In the international community, the principles, rules, procedures and institutions which in organised societies usually act as *transmitters* and filters do not seem to function adequately. In a society, moral obligations acquire their *effective power* and effective power and interests their *moral justification* through the social system. In this process rigid demarcations of obligation are softened and the powers of interest and coercion channelled into the confining but also relieving pipeline of the system, which continues to evolve from this interplay. Though this process, a consensus develops which regards social obligations as practical and necessary. The current chaotic condition of the international community may be ascribed in part to a total lack of any such common consensus. (I am deliberately avoiding any reference to a world public opinion as its existence is doubtful). However, there is a state of *common consciousness* that is shared by politicians and people of different states, and by widely varying social and cultural groups, which recognises that the world is in a critical state. This shared consciousness creates an area of communication.

The confusion pervading the international community is not caused primarily by incompatible ideas springing from opposing interest groups, social systems and ideologies, but by the completely conflicting answers which are given to vital questions relating to the identity of the international community, to the obligations which it can effectively carry out, and to its norms of behaviour. One viewpoint claims that there is no central power in the international community, only the unlimited self-interest of its components; and that, therefore, unlimited coercion is effective. This view does not allow for any moral obligations and regards power politics as natural and therefore right. This view is, in effect, the old tenet of vulgar Machiavellianism that it is the moral duty of the statesman to act in the interest of his country according to the law of the jungle. The Machiavellian outlook has lost favour in domestic policy, as it has become increasingly apparent that it is possible to govern in a way which is more moral, human and rational than was assumed in a system tailor-made for Caesar, Borgia. It would indeed be a step forward if the abandonment of Machiavellianism in national matters over the last 300 years could not be applied to the international scene.

Like a converse image of Machiavellianism, there also exists an equally popular viewpoint which applies high moral and ideal standards to every international resolution. Looking at the international situation from this stance, man is seen as more prone to think in terms of moral principles, political ideals and ideologies than at any other time in history. When justifying its actions and disputes, every state bombastically gives reasons and explanations based on the highest moral standards. If the opinion of the international community were unanimously and unequivocally that 'might is right', then such emotive justification would be ludicrous. After all in the past tyrants such as emperors and sultans exercising unlimited coercion never resorted to moral explanations.

Plenty of evidence exists for both the Machiavellian and the moral view. In numerous instances moral, political and social principles have been able to effect miraculous changes, cause the collapse of seemingly invincible power systems and create new states out of a void. On the other hand, there is no shortage of examples of instances where moral and idealistic considerations have become the tools of narrow self-interest or where, lacking the dynamic of self-interest, the most idealistic and intelligent of systems failed to function. Within individual societies, there exist more or less coherent theoretical and practical systems and methods to form one dialectic unit out of these two kinds of experiences, and so secure the practical effects of principles. Yet, when applied to the international community, the two schools immediately split and exist as thesis and antithesis. The Machiavellian camp naively attribute superhuman capabilities, possibilities and acts to selfish interests, brute force, tyranny, political cunning and sinister plots. Their moralistic opponents, of course, attribute equal powers to principles, ideals and institutions which embody them — such as the U.N. or international tribunals. In fact, self-interest and military power cannot manage without moral and idealistic justifications, nor can ideals and institutions function without an element of self-interest and power.

The two groups are not divided along the same lines as the opposing power groups, nor, necessarily, do peoples and governments apply one yardstick to themselves and another to the rest of the world. In this area, too, people and states seem to be schizophrenic, simultaneously adopting both opinions or vacillating between them. Sometimes the omnipotence of power is stressed because bitter experience has taught that high principles cannot be applied to modern politics, followed by a blind reversion to moral standards because people find that these are integral parts of all communities. It is also accepted that without some moral standards the world would be edging towards an abyss in which even tyranny could not serve its best interests. This schizophrenia exists even at the highest political levels. Consequently, we find a world in which there exists a policy of blind self-defence and power alongside a policy of rigid principle riddled with ideological slogans. These two seem incapable of being united in a synthesis that could be termed 'practical politics'.

The breakdown of public trust in the moral character of the international community has a surrealist quality, being totally at odds with the high-flown solutions to international problems that are widely propagated. Any of the solutions that claim to be of general validity or offer a total answer lack any practical guideline on how to achieve these high-minded goals. But the nub of the problem is exactly in this area. How *within* the framework of *actual possibilities* are modest but successful solutions to the *actual problems* to be found? Once some satisfactory temporary solutions are worked out then it will be possible to work on towards comprehensive answers. Therefore, we will confine our investigation to examining the peculiar *symptoms* and causes that underlie the paralysis of the international community and at the same time try to work out possible methods of over-powering the 'great fear' of our age *within* the *existing structures* and organisations. It is definitely not our intention to draft an abstract *Utopia* — we start with the assumption that for the foreseeable future the world will remain a collection of more or less sovereign states with stalemate among the great power groupings. Within this framework, we intend to draw up a *feasible Utopia* showing how the optimal functioning of the international community can be secured, taking into account the current features of that community. Then we intend to give examples of how such optimal functioning would affect the course of the problems that continue unresolved.

The following outlines are not a political criticism, nor a sociological description, nor a legal analysis of the international community, though all these elements will be present, but an examination of the balance and functioning of the international community. Political ideals, general principles, common convictions, legal organisations, procedures and rules, explicit and implicit conventions, balances of power, actual situations and the balance between all these factors will be given equal importance. In fact, we intend to examine not only the principle and blue-print of the machine, its sources of energy and its component parts, but also the lubricants which make all the difference between the smooth or jerky running of the machine.

[2]

The Structure and the Basic Governing Principles of the International Community

The problem of the legitimacy of power and of basic principles

Some people claim that there is no such thing as an international legality, and that in the international community each state is the natural enemy of every other state. If this interpretation is accepted, then people should not feel any unease or resentment when it seems that world peace is maintained mainly by transitory factors and a precarious balance of power. But we do find it hard to accept the current situation. This may be because for several centuries there has been a steadily growing movement aimed at transforming the community into a real legal entity based on a few fundamental and commonly held convictions and universally accepted procedures. At times in the past this movement has managed to create a practical political and moral balance, albeit with simpler legal formations than that which prevails today. In order to comprehend these phenomena it is vital to understand and define the complexities of the legitimacy of power, which is the fundamental problem of every properly organised community and legal system.

Social theorists have searched for centuries for a valid justification for the legitimacy of power – one that transcends mere fluctuating military supremacy or personal tyranny. Not surprisingly the forms of organisation, social structures, formulae of principles and theoretical tenets connected with this problem have not developed evenly or to the same degree in every culture. Often the political thought and social structure of very advanced cultures become arrested by exposure to brutal oppression. Sometimes the great thinkers in a society ignore the political and social events of their time and concentrate on more spiritual and transcendent matters. In two great cultures, the Graeco-Roman and the Chinese, both rulers and ruled defined the nature of power. In both societies, those in power felt compelled to find a justification for their rule, in addition to merely exercising and administering that power; and consequently, the masses who endured, supported or suspected the power élite were able to question it. Through this the idea of justifying power and of needing legitimacy for power became a decisive factor in these two cultures and a force which deeply affected other societies. Sometimes the ideas were used to justify the existing power, at other times to provoke mass risings and transform society through revolution. It is no historical chance that the most eminent and profound political philosophers in Greece, Rome and China were also involved in practical politics.

The ultimate basis for a claim to legitimate power is a common conviction that those exercising power are in fact competent to do so. It then follows that the people accept that the human attitudes, conditions and commands that are the products of power are in fact mandatory and reasonable: and also that the system of power distribution is right and practical. This common conviction is usually expressed in a few general and basic principles. The way in which these doctrines are expressed, their emphasis, phraseology and ideology may change through time and circumstances; but they always contain immediate statements on equality, loyalty, liberty and human dignity as opposed to unlimited power and tyranny. Among such basic principles are the divine right of kings, the sovereignty of the people, the decisive role of the nobility, of officialdom, the elders or the masses, the political principles of organisation which may claim supreme power for the people, the system of personal privileges, the principles of human rights, the principles of the limitation of the judiciary, etc.

These governing principles are not in themselves laws, but they are more than mere pious wishes or moral maxims. They are the formulation of the common conviction justifying or, possibly, criticising the rules or the effects of social organisation. At the same time they are the internal regulators of social organisation, compliance with them giving legitimacy to the actual legal system. They are norm-creating obligations and, at the same time, also the expressions of a general common conviction which accepts these obligations. They also become sociological facts simply because, in most cases, people believe in them. The basic principles go far beyond laws and differ from the legal rulings of codified law in that they simultaneously exert a justifying and a revolutionising, a consolidating and a subversive influence. But despite this shifting role, the basic principles exercise a greater and more profound durability for the legality they support than can be provided by any naked tyranny, no matter how strong that tyranny may seem. All that Barna Horvath has so correctly said of the justifying and revolutionary role of natural law can equally well be applied to the basic principles; indeed they are more real, more tangible than what is usually meant by natural law. This is why I have chosen to use the words 'basic governing principles', and I believe that it is because of the existence of basic principles that the idea of justifying power has spread throughout the world. At the present time the principles of sovereignty and self-determination are universally accepted, and so the justification of power has become the central question in the acquisition and retention of power — even on the international plane. So that even though we are moving further and further away from a situation in which power is exercised according to these basic principles it becomes ever more necessary to justify power in these terms.

The relationship between law, constitution and the basic governing principles

When a community feels the need to justify its own legitimacy through the affirmation of the basic principles, it is faced by a crucial dilemma. For the very apparatus of power that has been developed is derived from the set of common convictions now used to question it. No community with any degree of stability can, of course, afford to let this weighing-up of the governing principles happen too often. Most communities find some accepted format to ensure outward compliance with the basic principles which establishes them permanently. But this creates a certain tension between real compliance with the basic guiding principles, which is always open to question, and the formal procedures which establish the compliance. The essential material legitimacy of power derives from the community's acceptance of the basic principles which underlie the particular power structure and that constitutes its outward, formal legitimacy. Of course, neither the form nor the substance of legitimacy can exist alone; both are needed in varying degrees at different times. Without a minimum of defined form no system could survive, however, just its claims and acts. Conversely, no group can rule indefinitely if it is irrelevant and ineffective.

In order to resolve the conflict between essential and formal legitimacy, Europe and the New World evolved a method of regulation and evaluation. The essence of this method is that the various commands and acts issuing from authority are applied according to their chronological validity and their relative proximity to the basic principles. This means that the rules of the community can be debated, be the subject of conflict and ultimately be changed. However, there are a few rules which are so basic and important that they are regarded as unalterable and above every antagonism or dispute. Many individual states codify these exceptional basic laws into a constitution. Many constitutions contain a great deal that could be more flexible and omit a great deal that should be unalterable, due to the immediate political considerations or legal pedantry. The truly essential parts of the constitution are those which define the methods and institutions through which the basic principles will be realised. The method and processes of legislation, the appointment of public officers, the scope of power and its limitations, and the pattern of administration are laid down. In this way the justifying aspect of the basic principles is transmitted to the community, the legal system and the administration. So even if the basic principles are not specifically referred to in the constitution, they provide the framework for the life of the community; for if the basic principles were not adopted, the distinction between the articles of the constitution and the ordinary laws would be meaningless. If this does happen and a purely nominal hierarchy of laws evolves, the actual running of the community will remain merely a mass of amorphous, casual and arbitrary commands. If the constitution and ordinary laws spring from the same basic principles, rules are more likely to be accepted without constant scrutiny and so the community will be more stable. The soundness of the constitution and the acceptance of the power it represents will then justify all the secondary rules deriving from it. The legal banality that there is no such thing as an eternal law is also applied to refute the idea that there can be permanent articles of a constitution. In fact, however, it is only because of the institutional declaration that these articles are meant to be permanent and the dramatisation of the exceptional nature of any alteration, that the ordinary laws can be constantly renewed without causing any real upheaval. So the first problem in creating a constitution is that it must both comply with the basic principles and embody them if it is to be permanent and to create social stability. The basic principles have a critical as well as a justifying role. This critical function shows itself if the articles of the constitution are never fulfilled or if due to long application or social change, they become rigid, distorted or inadequate.

The second problem in the creation of constitutions is finding an answer to the contradiction of how to alter something meant to be permanent. How can the necessary exceptional alterations be made to the constitution if it is the foundation of communal order and if most people want it to be permanent? If the rules regulating change are too loose, communal order becomes liquid, anarchic and unstable. If the regulations are too rigid, either because change is thought sacrilegious or because no adequate procedure has been provided, communal order will become brittle, explosive and unstable. The most common solution is to accept that the rules relating to changing the articles of a constitution should be more difficult to fulfil than those relating to ordinary laws. In some cases it is left to a special body, in others a majority of two-thirds or three-quarters is required, in others special procedures, deadlines, repeated acceptance or a plebiscite are laid down.

If the object is simply to make the legal reflection of the common conviction in the constitution clearer, then the problem is surmountable. However, if the common conviction itself is in the process of changing and this change has to be reflected in the law or constitution, the problem is far more difficult. If the legitimacy of the legal system itself is being questioned, then any changes will be profound and probably painful.

This is why the relationship between the basic principles constituting the legitimacy of a legal system and the constitutional rules which express these principles, is double-edged. It is widely felt that to preserve the basis of the legal system fundamental constitutional institutions and procedures 'must not', 'should not', 'ought not' be disputed. Indeed, these matters are rarely disputed in a stable structure, not because it is forbidden or frowned upon, but because these basic institutions are preserved, not by prohibitions but by a common conviction that takes them for granted. If this common conviction dries up or if it is shaken, no prohibitive measures or official disapproval can mask the fact that something is wrong with the entire legal system. While the common conviction is intact, the sacred legitimacy of the ultimate principles and basic institutions can be taken for granted and any opposition can be condemned as subversive. If public opinion, however, begins to doubt the very basis of the legal system, then these doubts make it necessary to reassess the whole legal system.

The territorial status of states and the 'constitution' of the international community

The basic 'articles of the constitution' held by the international community are difficult to pinpoint. While it is possible that the Charter of the U.N. may at some time in the future become such an instrument, that is far from the case at the present time. The followers of Hans Kelsen claim that the 'constitution' of the international community is the assumption that treaties are binding (*pacta sunt servanda*). However, this very general and formal viewpoint states little more than that 'the laws must be observed' and that in international law the characteristic form of a legal rule is the international treaty. While this is both true and important, true constitutions are not a collection of formal rules but embody in their rules and procedures common convictions and loyalties. A constitution will prescribe the form of government; it will lay down the line of succession and the privileges that exist in the community, and name the class in possession of those privileges; it will, furthermore, state the rights of the people, the forms in which the sovereign will of the people may show itself, etc. However, international law currently has few of these characteristics, only a few simple principles concerned with certain fundamental rights of sovereign states, treaties between states, and constitutions of new states.

Any analogy between the regulated constitution of individual states and any order in the international community is hard to justify. However, a more useful starting point might be the incoherent and loose tie that binds the world community of nations and the territorial status which draws the demarcation lines between them, i.e. national frontiers. These are some kind of 'golden mean' to the international community and it is a shared assumption that these are unalterable. If the territorial integrity of states was not a permanent factor, not easily changed, many of the most fundamental notions of international law would flounder. Among such fundamental rules are the distinction between the mother country and foreign nations; nationals and foreign citizens; domestic and foreign laws; internal and foreign policy; domestic issues and foreign intervention. It is in order to preserve their security, independence and territorial integrity that most countries undertake willingly the limitations and responsibilities that an international legal system imposes upon them. When countries appeal to international legality, it is usually because either their independence or their territorial integrity is threatened. As recognised borders are generally sacrosanct, any change ranks as an exceptional instance which will only be accepted in rare circumstances.

However, while territorial changes are regarded as exceptional, the legal procedures needed to sanction the territorial changes that result from wars or agreement are readily available and have been frequently used. The only rule in international law, as it exists today, is that territories must be conceded by international treaty. In effect, therefore, national frontiers come under the same legal framework that controls frontier control, postal agreements, or foreign trade. It is only since the First World War, the emergence of the League of Nations and then that of the U.N. that the political arms of these international agencies have taken decisions over certain insignificant local questions of state formation or territorial changes, and even these were basically contractual agreements.

It is ironic that international law is so underdeveloped that the vague set of rules regulating changes in states and their territories (which is the nearest we come to an international constitution) is both too loose and too rigid, compared with the highly articulate legal systems of individual states. International law is too loose because a change can be effected through an ordinary treaty, and too rigid because in the absence of particular legal procedures designed for the purpose, any effort to change or constitute a new state are invariably resisted vehemently by the states directly concerned. This being so, the usual method of altering frontiers in 'exceptional circumstances' has been war. The number of occasions where revised frontiers resulted from compromise, peaceful bargaining or international arbitration is depressingly small.

The myth of the unlimited power of naked strength and territorial sovereignty

Whether it is a peace treaty after war or a treaty deriving from the decision of international policy agencies that causes the alteration of the territorial *status quo,* naked coercion or overwhelming power has always played an important part in decisions relating to territory. However, when one views dispassionately the history of the community of European states and the international community which sprang from it, it is clear that territorial changes which follow military coercion have not always happened as a matter of course. Since the emergence of a stable European community in the ninth to eleventh centuries, the concept of justifying power has also been applied to changes in territorial *status quo*. Even changes brought about by war remained largely within the framework of the basic principles which have been the fundamental basic principles of state and social organisation and also of the division of territory in Europe. Not surprisingly these principles have been subjected to different interpretations by the contestants, but in essence they have never been doubted. In the Middle Ages, the basic principles were based on feudal and dynastic rights; this led to the principles embodied in the divine right of kings, which were in turn replaced by the rights of nations, the nationality principle and more recently the principle of self-determination. Of course, running concurrently with all these principles has been a certain balancing of power. War has always been an exceptional, dramatic event which shocked both the emotions and conscience of Europeans, even when in international law it was accepted as the natural method of settling territorial disputes. Even then, the decision to make war was usually painstakingly justified in terms of the prevalent basic principles. The justifications ranged from dynastic claims and historical legitimacy, the restoration of the European balance and struggle for national unity, to an attempt to secure the rights of self-determination, the liberation of oppressed peoples, colonies and so on. Following a victory, the settlements were always framed in terms of these principles, even if the drafting of details was influenced by arbitrary, capricious and immediate factors.

When the commonly accepted principles are no longer respected and states merely pay lip-service to them or cynically ignore them, this is a sure sign of demoralisation or disintegration. The cynical wars launched by Frederick the Great for the possession of Silesia and the partition of Poland foreshadowed the Napoleonic overthrow of the established order in Europe. In the first quarter of our century, when international treaties were referred to as 'mere scraps of paper', when *'sacro egoismo'* became the order of the day, when declarations of war (which were simply political manoeuvrings) became fashionable, the great global political chaos of modern times was developing. In such periods of critical transition, the theory of the 'state not bound by any norm save its own interest' appears; but even this theory, diametrically opposed to the great European tradition that both power and its use must be justified, has itself to be justified. The followers of the 'might is right' school advanced grandiose claims that it was the only realistic attitude, whereas in fact it is merely an exaggerated generalisation of a disillusioned recognition that violence has a significant role in both internal and external affairs. It is notable that the most avid supporters of the idea of the immoral state and total war are theoreticians and not generals or rulers. Those who actually wield power are usually happy to return to a system in which action is limited by principles, after they have experienced a few disastrous episodes outside such an order. There have been several attempts to dominate Europe totally by a victorious tyrant — Napoleon, the Hohenzollerns, Hitler — all of which ended disastrously and were followed by the reintroduction of policies based on principle. Permanent territorial rearrangements have only been possible in compliance with the basic principles. The idea of the necessity, both logical and practical, to justify power has become accepted throughout the world, even if it is not always put into practice. Even imperialist wars and colonial rule, which were launched and maintained by motives far more cynical and unscrupulous than the accepted norms of Europe, had to find justification and, failing to do so, have become unjustifiable and unacceptable.

The most important aspect of the constitution of the international community relates to territorial status, which cannot be changed arbitrarily or unlimitedly, although the legal forms for effecting such changes are still embryonic.

[3]

The Principles Governing Monarchic-Feudal Legitimacy

The old community of European states

It was stated earlier that the international legal community is a primitive and unstable organisation, but this is not a necessary combination of characteristics. Some communities with a primitive organisation are stable. This was the case in the Middle Ages, for instance, when, despite the numerous manifestations of anarchy and brute force, feudal and dynastic relationships were highly durable and resistant to change. In the seventeenth and eighteenth centuries, the principle of monarchic-feudal legitimacy could create a relatively high level of stable European order. This order had, as shown by Guglielmo Ferrero, its own legitimate base – the divine right of kings. However, this legitimacy was never universally accepted and opposition developed at the beginning of the modern era, which in due course merged with revolutionary movements aimed at the destruction of absolute monarchy. But in the area of inter-state relations, absolute monarchy made it possible for an extremely simple and stable international constitution to evolve, based on the convention that international treaties were sufficient to sanction territorial change.

The sovereign was free to cede part of his territories as it was held that he had the right to dispose of the loyalties of his subjects. The subjects accepted this tradition and when Francis of Lorraine ceded some of his hereditary lands to Stanislav Lesczynski, the people wept as he bade them farewell; yet they accepted a succession of new rulers compliantly, for under the prevailing system they owed loyalty to the new sovereign. War was the only means of settling a territorial dispute, and from the mid-seventeenth century up to the French Revolution, warfare became formalised in the manner of a duel. In comparison with later wars the destructive impact was limited by fighting with small professional armies and war was not intended to annihilate the enemy. Kings were not only blood relatives but also comrades 'under the skin'. In any event they were members of the same community and, despite national differences, they had a strong sense of affinity. The victor did not go to extremes in exploiting his military triumph and was usually satisfied with a favourable settlement of the original dispute – the defeated would give up the disputed area and in most cases resign himself to the new situation. So war really did 'settle the matter'. As late as the mid-nineteenth century, Franz-Joseph was able to settle matters with Napoleon III, after the Battle of Solferino, by giving up a province. Also, where the will to avert war existed, the system of territorial exchange was a useful tool. This was first attempted by William III of England in order to avert the War of the Spanish Succession. The method was successfully applied throughout the eighteenth century and was elaborated at the Congress of Vienna. In a world where a subject's loyalty was negotiable and transferable, public opinion saw no harm in exchanging territory without consulting the inhabitants. In addition, as the territorial exchange system often succeeded in averting wars, it was ranked as one of civilisation's achievements.

As long as the formal legal distribution of land was based on the theory of monarchic-feudalism, there were few contradictions between actuality and legitimacy and loyalty. If contradictions did arise, they could be settled by an appropriate peace treaty. The rule for instituting new states was equally simple, recognition by the rest of the community being the sole test of validity. This was straightforward – the sovereigns and the remaining aristocratic republics signified their acceptance of the new sovereign into the community.

Even in countries with a constitution that limited the power of the monarch and supported the freedoms of the nobility or citizens, the sovereigns were able to control foreign affairs and to be part of the legal order of European absolutism. England, Holland, Sweden and Switzerland thrived on the system and succeeded in exploiting it to gain territory. Other nations, such as Belgium in 1714 and Norway in 1814, merely tolerated it and gave their belated assent to decisions made without them. Others again, like Poland, Hungary, Bohemia and Ireland, found that they had to stand alone without the support of a dynasty at crucial moments in their national history, and were thus defeated or crippled. Not until new principles of national self-determination evolved did these countries have any redress.

The European network of monarchic absolutism reached its zenith in the second half of the seventeenth century. Even after the French Revolution and the Napoleonic Wars this system continued to provide the background to the comparatively peaceful and prosperous years from the Congress of Vienna to the First World War.

The disintegration of monarchic-feudal legitimacy and its restoration

The first signs of disintegration showed themselves in the eighteenth century in three different ways. The first factor came from within the community itself, when certain rulers resorted to the use of the military weapon with total cynicism and considerable success. This process started with the Silesian wars of Frederick the Great and reached its climax in the partition of Poland, which is still exerting an adverse affect on European stability.

The second factor was the growth of a new ideology. The divine right of kings was being questioned and replaced by ideas of popular sovereignty, freedom and equality. Following inevitably from this was the collapse of the concept of feudal dues which saw the loyalty of an individual as owing to the person of the sovereign or to the treaties he saw fit to make. All these new ideas were embodied in the French Revolution, during which the idea of the right to self-determination first emerged, and plebiscites were first attempted, even if the motives were not entirely lacking in self-interest. Furthermore, a new focus of loyalty emerged — the nation. The nation was seen as an integral unit inspiring democratic fervour among its loyal citizens. The modern concept of national identity derived from the heightened intensity of mass emotion. Naturally the divine right of kings was an early victim of this new-found national and democratic feeling. It was only after the Revolutionary and Napoleonic Wars that a more inward-looking and hermetic variety of nationalism developed which did not always see the nation and universal freedom as synonymous.

The third factor was the growth of the theory of total war and of a technology that facilitated its practice. The theory of total war first appeared in eighteenth- and nineteenth-century literature on military matters in opposition to the mannered and limited 'frivolous' wars of the seventeenth and eighteenth centuries. Theories of total war rejected the civilising influence of limited war, which itself had developed as a reaction to the Thirty Years' War, an earlier form of total warfare. The revival of unlimited war theories was paralleled by the revival of Machiavellian practices by sovereigns. Ironically, however, it was in the Revolutionary Wars following the French Revolution that compulsory military service was introduced leading to total warfare, and it was subsequently spread throughout Europe by the Napoleonic War. Revolutionary ideology, indeed, became tainted by its association with protracted and bloody wars.

The Congress of Vienna had little trouble in imposing the system of monarchic legitimacy on a war-weary Europe. As Ferrero so accurately points out, it was at this time that the enormously intricate web of legitimate territorial changes was contrived within the framework of a unified monarchic European 'Common Law'. The crux of the system was that all territory held without legal justification must be returned to its legitimate ruler and that the only legitimate method of such change was through orderly treaties between their rulers. The fate of such territories as were left without legitimate rulers would be decided by the community of

European rulers. So it was within this framework that the Congress of Vienna successfully applied the conciliatory mode of territorial changes, though even at the time there was an outcry over the lack of concern for and consultation with the inhabitants affected. Such criticisms had not been heard over exchanges prior to the French Revolution. However, the real areas of failure of the Congress of Vienna occurred where they did not consistently apply their own basic principles. The principle of legitimacy was so narrowly applied that, apart from Switzerland and a few German free cities, hereditary monarchies were the only ruling caste to be restored, the elected monarchies and republics being left dormant.

So the awesome legacies of the Congress of Vienna were the contradictory state of the German body politic and the continuation of the partition of Poland which heralded the end of the eighteenth-century balance. The reckoning came, after a hundred years of comparative peace following the Congress, with the World Wars which shattered Europe; and they occurred because of the immaturity of the German political system and the uncertain status of the Polish state.

The settlements made by the Congress of Vienna were, however, no mean achievement. Its greatest success was the frequent gathering together of the leading European statesmen which was necessitated by the principles laid down at the Congress. This led to the 'European Concert of Powers' of the nineteenth century, which involved repeated meetings or diplomatic correspondence between the foreign ministers of initially the five, but later the six, leading powers. This Concert decided disputes over territories or over the formation of new states. The method was suprisingly successful, once it overcame the odium attached to the Holy Alliance, and in spite of, or maybe because of, its primitive procedures, Belgian independence was achieved relatively easily, the repeated Balkan crises were quickly defused and the emerging Balkan nations launched on the road to independence, a few wars were averted and others localised. All in all, the 'Concert of Europe' was not unsuccessful until 1914.

The relationship between monarchic-feudal legitimacy and the principle of nationhood

Despite the efforts at conciliation made by the Congress of Vienna, the old regimes never quite recovered from the blow dealt by the French Revolution. In the nineteenth century diplomacy reverted once more to the monarchs and nobility of Europe, who returned to the tradition of limited warfare with small professional armies. Prussia alone continued with compulsory national service, Prussia was humiliatingly demilitarised in 1806, and enthusiastically rearmed in 1813, seeing this act as a revival of national glory. It was only when the Prussian army scored such easy and overwhelming victories later in the nineteenth century that the other nations of Europe felt compelled to compete in the arms race. At the same time as setting the military pace, Prussia succeeded France as the trouble-maker of Europe. However, the shape of Europe was not decided by the, monarchies alone — they, if they could have managed it, would have abolished war altogether or found a way of limiting it yet further. It is notable that none of the wars of the nineteenth century were fought over legal or dynastic claims but were mainly caused by 'national' questions. The 'nationality' question raged in the nineteenth century in Central and Eastern Europe because, unlike Western Europe, the nation states did not develop within historical frontiers, and national aspirations contradicted the existing dynastic framework.

The growth of national consciousness and revolt in the nineteenth century occurred in two waves: first, former national units which were either dissolved or suppressed by the dynasties, such as Germany, Italy, Poland, Hungary, Bohemia and Greece emerged; this was followed by the more vehement demands by groups which claimed nationhood on linguistic and ethnic origins. By the middle of the nineteenth century, the principle of the 'nation' took shape and through the policies of Napoleon III became a new governing principle. There were a few plebiscites, but in general controversies involving nationalism were settled through the rules and procedures of the dynastic system. If a national uprising became too violent to be contained by the dynastic system, the cause was invariably taken up by another dynasty, and following a decisive military victory the revolt was either quelled or a new nation emerged. Whichever dynasty had backed the new state gained status and often territory for itself. The concert of powers made sure that the new states fitted into the old order by instituting new dynasties, as in the cases of Belgium, unified Italy, Bismark's Germany, the Balkan states and independent Norway. However, the thorny problem of divided Poland and the nations under the Hapsburg monarchies remained unresolved. This system, though seemingly successful, was essentially schizophrenic and ultimately it corrupted both the dynasties and the national movements. Dynasties such as the Hapsburgs and the Romanovs were corrupted because their framework was not compatible with national movements. The new 'national' dynasties such as the German and Italian monarchies had betrayed the old dynastic loyalties by the very fact of their existence and therefore felt ambivalent towards the dynastic system. Every dynasty in Europe either opposed or identified with a nationalist struggle and had reason therefore to fear the strengthening of popular national movements. This fear led to increasingly unrealistic, adventurous and treacherous policies, which were motivated by both self-preservation and expansive 'national policies'.

The national movements were themselves corrupted both by the uncertainty of their territorial status and by the continuing acceptance in international law of territorial change without consultation of the peoples concerned. Instances where such changes no longer complied with volatile public opinion increased. A situation steadily emerged in which it was no longer a question of an oppressive sovereign against an oppressed nation, but of confrontations between the oppressive and oppressed nation state. Also, in the struggle for national unity it sometimes became necessary to seek the support of a repressive dynasty in order to survive, and in this situation the close connnection between national evolution and progressive liberal politics was reduced. Loyalty towards dynasties which had aided national causes was at times so overwhelming and unquestioning that anti-libertarian cults and expectations actually developed around certain monarchs or dynasties.

By the second half of the nineteenth century compulsory military service was accepted throughout Europe. In military matters modern methods of mass organisation were grotesquely intermingled with the old traditions of dynastic warfare: the aristocratic attitudes of the officer class somehow fused with memories of the French Revolutionary Wars, the halo of Napoleonic traditions and the ideology of national interest unrestrained by moral inhibitions.

The outbreak of the First World War and the collapse of monarchic-feudal legitimacy

By the beginning of the twentieth century conditions in Central and Eastern Europe were ripe for change. Causes for this lay in the unprincipled and schizophrenic way in which questions had been settled and in the neglect of the roots of the problems in the otherwise largely successful European settlement of 1815.

In the field of foreign policy, especially, both the national movements and the dynasties were in error. In those very countries where dynasties were exalted as the founders of national unity and the guardians of national territory and where democratic development was halted, the rulers retained almost unlimited control in foreign affairs; and this was so even in those countries with some measure of parliamentary practice. Some rulers were virtually free of all parliamentary control – free in their choice of advisors on foreign policy, in their choice of generals, in decisions of peace and war. The national movements were resigned to allowing their sovereigns to make decisions about the nation's chief interests without democratic controls. The rulers on their part, for all their very real powers, were at their wits' ends. Their privileges, duties and responsibilities in matters of war were both a spur and a restraint. They were unaware of their ability to make decisions different from those they actually made, and they had lost the courage to conduct their foreign policies in their own old, well-established, limited but successful way, serving their own dynastic goals according to their own rights. They allowed 'national' interests to determine their policies, believing these interests to be supported by the irresistible power of the masses, a power they felt they must come to terms with if they were to retain their dynastic future in this revolutionary, democratic world, made so 'confused' by nationalist ideas. Yet the ideologies which defined national objectives and interests were in most cases no longer the great and irresistible movements of nation-formation and sovereignty of the people, but were caught in a confusion of self-contradictory sentiments of nationalism, without form and still dominated by the spirit of autocracy and oligarchy. Although they were part of the public awareness they had nothing like the massive force of the original movements for national freedom. Both rulers and nations were motivated by a sense of uncertainty, partly from the threats to their existence and partly from the idiosyncratic nature of their alliance with each other, but neither had any interest in or liking for war. However, to compensate for their uncertainties, both dynasties and national movements put on a display of sword-rattling, fictitious resoluteness.

In contrast to this the foreign policies of the Western democracies were based on realities and not on fiction. In these countries national interests, whether well- or ill-conceived, were the deciding influence in their policies, the dynasties having long since lost their decisive role. Fear of German domination and warmongering pushed these democracies first into a system of alliance and later into war, while they failed to understand the great national and social witches' cauldron behind the facade of threats and prestige postures of the autocracies and semi-autocracies. At the same time arms manufacturers keen on profit, generals keen on promotion and ideologists keen on national glory seized on the possibilities and prepared, advertised and conducted the war following their own almost blind laws.

Never before, perhaps, was a war fought in such utter confusion as regards its ultimate goals. Apart from Serbia and Belgium, there was hardly a country, hardly a people that knew what it was fighting for. The semi-autocracies of Central Europe appealed to their nations to fight what they literally regarded as the freemasonry of the Western democracies, appealed under the unlikely cloak of a holy war on the tyranny of the Czars. The Western democracies, in turn, asked their people to conduct a holy war against German autocracy, but in alliance with the Czar. As for the more practical aims of each country, territorial claims, deriving from well-defined national considerations, thus lost much of their persuasive power as the sufferings caused by the war became less and less bearable, not to mention the delirious daydreams which had never represented any true national interests and which, for want of anything more realistic, the empires of the three great dynasties began to set up as their goals: for Russia it was Istanbul; for Austro-Hungary, the entire Balkans; for Germany, the whole of Central Europe and the Ukraine, etc.

It was the world's misfortune that it had to be this war, fought with no clear purposes, which was to be the first major European war not dependent on small professional armies. Instead, general and compulsory military service — with the exception of Great Britain where the moral pressure of society first forced men to volunteer — drew almost entire populations into the fight, huge masses of peaceful and ordinary people who would at best have been able to endure and support no more than a few months of war. But the fight was dreadfully prolonged by the newly advanced techniques of warfare and especially by the largely defensive character of trench warfare imposed by the newly invented machine-gun. Therefore, in order to keep up morale, propaganda was used to represent the entire race of the enemy as monsters. Those who did not believe the propaganda, perhaps on account of their experiences at the front, were more and more inclined to regard, among the more hidden causes, those truly responsible as the monsters.

So the war soon got far beyond either the understanding or the control of those who launched it. It posed so many national and social problems, shaking authorities, destroying and impoverishing masses and stirring up such emotions that in the end the great Central and Eastern European dynasties were completely destroyed, taking with them the entire monarchic-feudal order. Unlike the situation at the time of the Congress of Vienna, when the fall of Napoleonic militarism was a justification and triumph for traditional monarchy, this time militarism and monarchism were both compromised and they fell together.

[4]

The Right of Self-Determination as the New Basic Principle of Order

Self-determination and the question of responsibility for the war

With the collapse of monarchic-feudal legitimacy, a new formula was needed. The old framework of international law was still valid, and within it both war and international treaties were acceptable means of acquiring new territory. But now this framework had become an empty skeleton. The convictions which had given it life and validity were dead. A war that involved calling millions of peaceful citizens to arms could no longer be described as a means to an end — it was a catastrophe; while, with the increased power of public opinion in modern society, the loyalty of citizens was not transferable simply by international treaty.

The new basis of state-formation and territorial settlements was 'the principle of the self-determination of the people'. This had been established through the French Revolution, but now, after the First World War, and together with the principle of sovereignty of the people within the state, the idea of self-determination was to become a ruling force, replacing the old ideas of loyalty to the sovereign and to monarchic-feudal legitimacy. It seemed that these new principles could retroactively justify the awful war which, after the fall of Czarism and the entry of the United States, seemed to become something more akin to a fight between the democracies and the autocracies. But the new Soviet State was to deny this: it lumped together the Western democracies and the defeated Central European semi-autocracies as capitalist and bourgeois systems. However, in the principle of self-determination there was a common basis that satisfied almost everyone. It answered the new democratic and nationalistic demands and desire for autonomy and unity in Central and Eastern Europe, and it answered the declared intentions of both the new Soviet and the United States. It was therefore almost unopposed.

If a democratic international community was to emerge on the basis of the principle of self-determination, the solidarity of kings had to be replaced by the solidarity of self-governing peoples; and they who could no longer view war as a polite duel, and who had achieved peace through the commonly accepted new principles and methods, must create a system in which all new controversies could be settled without war. Such was the concept of the same high-minded public opinion that had formulated the principle of self-determination. But the people wanted all the solidarity and trust formerly shown by the kings. Around 1848 they had it, when the main emphasis was on domestic reform and the chief antagonists were kings versus peoples. But by 1918 the antagonists had become nations set against their political systems. The fact that the United States, the main victor, was not directly involved in the European controversies would have made it possible for President Wilson to take the useful role of arbiter at the peace conference, but he was forced to give way to the short-term interests of the European powers. Aggressive nationalism saw in the new settlement a kind of law of the jungle, every nation opposed to the others. But the main defeat was caused by the frightful mass emotions that sought to punish the criminals responsible for launching this senseless war.

There were three theories about who was responsible for the war. The first and simplest was that the blame fell on the defeated European combatants, who were thus expected to pay the bill run up by sword-rattling emperors and generals. This idea underlay the whole Treaty of Versailles. It forbade them to keep a large army – which immediately made an army seem desirable and essential rather than a burden; it topped the serious points with strict demands that were never taken literally, such as the extradition of the Emperor and of officers who had committed war crimes; and it made petty stipulations such as the ruling that the Germans must not call their champagnes 'Champagner'. All this was then sanctioned by a treaty admitting the Germans' responsibility for the war, and as a result produced communal hysteria leading to those very atrocities in the Second World War for which the German nation felt it had been unjustly blamed in the First.

The second and the most comprehensive and convincing theory was put forward by the socialists and communists. For them the real responsibility for the war lay with imperialism, more specifically its twin motive forces of monopolistic capitalism and the bourgeoisie. This explanation satisfied the masses because of their deep hatred for the war profiteers: the war had been useful to them, so they must have caused it. Although this was an oversimplification, it gave birth to an extremely constructive concept for peace negotiations: the concept of the new Soviet State based on self-determination, of a peace without annexations and reparations. But this, along with Wilson's ideas, was in opposition to the plans of the European victors. From this clash, the resulting wars of intervention in Russia, the subsequent isolation of the Soviet Union, and from class interests, ideological dogmatism and a crusading attitude, East and West took to regarding each other as the very embodiment of the devil. As a result, only short-term reconciliation based on momentary identity of interests was possible between bourgeois democracy and socialism. This mutual hostility prevented, on the one hand, the constructive governing principles of the Soviet State and, on the other, the principles of self-determination and world organisation of President Wilson, from joining in a common action against the primitive and short-sighted 'realpolitik' of the victors. It took fascism — unfortunately the full-fledged form of it — to show up some common values beyond their momentary common interests, and then only for a short while.

The third theory of liability for the war, widespread in East, and West, blamed secret diplomacy. It was mainly directed against those secret pacts that were forerunners of the contesting groups of alliances and later determined the post-war settlements. There was nothing unusual in these pacts within the old, monarchistic international law; but it was precisely because they reflected the two most outmoded points of the old law, the right to wage war and the right to transfer territories without consulting the people, that they were so violently disliked. Indignant public opinion denounced all forms of secrecy, not only in basic principles and treaties, but also in the negotiations leading up to the treaties. And this, of course, is just not possible. This pressure, resulting in pseudo- and semi-publicity, only added to the difficulties of the peace negotiations without really making them more democratic.

All these attitudes helped to create a situation that was not helpful to the new governing principle of self-determination, yet self-determination remained the decisive force of state-formation and the new order, and together with the ethnic principle, it prevented the realisation of certain totally arbitrary plans. It was applied in broad outline only, while detail was determined by quarrels of nationalism, unprincipled compromise and brief-lived balances of power. Thus the Turks, because of a local war, became partial victors over the Greeks, whilst in a few cases vanquished countries managed to enforce plebiscites. The position of the national minorities resulting from the post-war frontiers of all East European countries was meant to be governed by special laws on minorities. In the Middle East and the colonial world the distribution of conquered lands was settled by the bargains driven between the European colonial powers. As a concession to the Wilsonian principles, the institution of the mandate, later trusteeship, was created, and this, in a roundabout and rather arbitrary way, led to independence coming sooner in most of the territories concerned than in other colonial territories.

There was no question of peace treaties being made through the consistent application of the principle of self-determination and all it entails: impartial procedures, plebiscites, decisions by impartial agencies. The treaties remained traditional in form, but without the main virtues of the traditional, secret negotiations of the monarchies, that is without the unemotional atmosphere and the close and confident relationship between the parties. This can be seen in the almost schizophrenic texts of these peace treaties. Side by side were set down the conditions of peace, drafted under the influence of short-term 'realpolitik', anger, pettiness and special interests, and the Charter of the League of Nations outlining a generous new order based on the solidarity of the people. This is the general political schizophrenia in which, brief intervals of reason apart, mankind still exists.

The balance-sheet after the first application of self-determination

The new European order thus contained contradictions when measured against its professed principles of self-determination, contradictions not present in the old order where the right of people to self-determination was simply not an issue. So the inter-war period was one of endless recriminations over right or wrong applications of self-determination, and sterile dispute between those powers which insisted on the *status quo* and those which, on the basis of eternal dynamism, demanded revision of the new frontiers. Statutes on the rights of minorities in Central and Eastern European peace treaties failed to avert these disputes. The statutes were intended to channel the discontents which would follow the redrafting of the map, but the countries concerned viewed them as an encroachment on their sovereignty, favouring their disloyal citizens. They saw the statutes as levers of the movements demanding territorial changes. Minorities living near the borders did not see why the principle of self-determination should force them to become citizens of a country to which they had no loyalties. In the long run tensions springing from these feelings joined with the hysterical mass movements which helped Hitler to power. Hitler first appeared as the champion of the right of genuine self-determination, only to become its gravedigger in the Second World War. This was the extent of the consolidation which the peace treaties were able to achieve.

The period of the post-war settlements was one of those great moments of fluidity which are sudden turning points for eras that have become stagnant or unchanging in direction. Such historical moments can point to new directions valid for a long time to come. These are moments when every course seems a possible one, and it can be enlightening to speculate on what could have happened. It is not that we can change the past, but an analysis of the situations can help us understand their effect on history; and this at a time when ideals and principles are increasingly important. When events reflect reason we see everything as lucid, natural, dictated by necessity; and when we find them governed by a confusion of short-term interests and passions, we can feel bitter over missed chances. The Congress of Vienna was such a moment in history. Then the largely consistent application of Talleyrand's formulation of monarchic legitimacy laid the cornerstone of European stability that lasted for a hundred years.

Yet by settling certain questions wrongly, it left a legacy of unresolved questions that would aid its eventual overthrow.

What then would have happened if, after the First World War, Wilson and the new Soviet State could have co-operated to force though a consistent application of the right to self-determination? How would it have been if, in 1919, the Soviet gospel of self-determination and peace without annexation and reparations had been taken seriously? The most remarkable result — and one that would have understandably shaken the victors — would have been the enlargement of Germany by the Anschluss of Austria, who at that time apparently wanted such a union. At the same time Germany would probably have lost as much territory in the East as she in fact lost as a result of the Versailles Treaty — perhaps without the correcting effect of the plebiscite in Silesia — but ultimately she would have gained something significant after losing the war. A decisive consequence of this German gain might have been the birth of a viable Eastern European federation as a counterbalance to the increased power of Germany. But the most decisive effect of such a settlement would have been psychological. The gain Germany would have owed to self-determination could have reversed that erroneous historical experience: that the road to greatness and unity led through 'blood and iron'. So the great German hysteria, together with the other major and minor nationalistic manias, either would never have risen or would have been much milder, and it is almost certain that there would have been no fascism on a European scale, and no Second World War. Also the frontier between Poland and the Soviet Union could have been much as it is today. In addition, if the policies had been based on reason and principle, there would have been no intervention in Russia, therefore the Russian Civil War would have been a much smaller affair, and so, probably, the isolation of the Soviet Union from the rest of Europe would have been briefer, and the face shown towards Europe a different one.

Of course, this guessing game may also be reversed. We could say that it was a merciful miracle that an American President in a decisive position raised the banner of self-determination when that was precisely what Europe most needed, and that this principle was up to a point carried through. If all principles had been pushed aside to allow the most brutish and unprincipled power interests to determine the events of the future, then France would have taken the entire Rhineland from Germany and would have tried to break Germany into small parts; Italy would have been given a far larger slice of what is now Yugoslavia; Hungary might have been completely divided; and the intervention in Russia would have been pursued with far greater vigour. The monstrous political hysterias that this would have created are beyond imagination — although it is hard to think of anything worse than Hitlerism. In any case the Second World War would have broken out sooner or later.

So far as the ultimate results are concerned, it appears that the difference between a complete lack of principle and its partial application is less than the difference between either of these two and a policy consistently based on principles.

Self-determination after the Second World War

The effects of the Second World War, in which sufferings and shock were even far greater than in the First, cast a compromising shadow over the principle of self-determination. However one analysed the tragic aspects of the war, sooner or later one encountered the theme of self-determination. It was easy to reach the oversimplified conclusion that the principle of self-determination could not produce a stable settlement, or that it was an instrument of fascist-inspired subversion, or that it could not be applied consistently; but it was rarely said that the principle was no longer valid. In fact, for the first time in history it was laid down in a comprehensive international document – the Charter of the United Nations – becoming one of its basic tenets.

But in Europe it had become somewhat suspect to appeal too loudly to the principle of self-determination: it was not mentioned quite so often in the course of the peace negotiations; and whenever it was mentioned it was referred to with less passion; nor was the system of minority statutes codified in the new treaties. On the other hand, there was one paradoxical effect of the principle: since the treaties which stipulated territorial transfers did not include safeguards for the loyalty of the inhabitants involved, population exchange was seen as a means of securing lasting possession of these territories.

But the movement towards self-determination worked with elemental force against the colonial powers, who increasingly lost the ability and the courage to retain their colonies either in the name of conquest or racial superiority. The great determination of the colonial peoples themselves in their struggle for freedom was of great importance, particularly those non-violent actions identified with the name of Gandhi. But it was also remarkable that the opposition to the struggle for liberation by the majority of colonial powers was less than wholehearted and towards the end of the process most of them showed a great measure of co-operation in liberating the territories – a brand-new development in the long and bloody history of colonial conquest. Admittedly this liberal attitude often had a touch of bad faith in it, frequently showing glee over the chaos which was bound to follow withdrawal; but the entire process could not have happened as it did but for the acceptance of the democratic principles of sovereignty of the people and self-determination. These fostered a significant antipathy towards colonial rule and a decreased 'will to rule'. It is therefore short-sighted to suppose that this willingness to release their colonies was mainly due to defeat, compulsion, self-interest or a shrewd change of tactics, although these had some part to play.

If these had been the decisive factors, it is hard to explain why Portugal, economically and militarily the weakest colonial power, should have been the least compelled to make concessions and so capable of resisting any attempt at freedom by her colonies. Certainly her determination to rule, international intrigues and great power hypocrisy played a part; but it is a simpler and sufficient explanation to say that the Portuguese style of domestic government is autocratic, and so it is natural for her to refuse to recognise the right to self-determination for her colonies as well as for her own people. When we say that Portuguese colonial power cannot maintain itself much longer, we have at least as much reason to expect that the collapse of this colonial rule will come from the general collapse of autocracy in Portugal as from military or economic failure.

After colonial self-determination

The comparatively liberal attitude of the colonial powers was sadly diminished by the efforts to keep their political and economic influence within the new countries rather than by giving priority to stability, which would have served more far-reaching ends. So the new triumphal march to self-determination took place under circumstances as chaotic as the earlier one. Colonial liberation created some fifty new states in Asia, Africa and the Western hemisphere, their formation reflecting the right to self-determination without any advance in the technique of applying the principle. The territorial settlements and emergence of the new states were effected by the existing positions of power of the colonies and liberation movements. The new borders were drawn along the lines of the frontiers between the colonies, fixed at the time of their original conquest, or along the internal frontiers between the administrative districts within a colony, as though it went without saying that these borders would automatically become the frontiers of the new nations.

Some of these nations had their own, clearly recognisable national identity. Others already showed a fairly well-developed modern political consciousness within their basic ethnic and tribal cohesion. There were some where the international or administrative borders drawn by the former colonial powers could make feasible national frontiers. But these factors received little consideration at the time of liberation. Some plebiscites were conducted over rather casually created territorial units, relating to immediate interests or positions of strength, but quite often the alternatives given to the voters were inadequate or even posed in bad faith. Occasionally, so as to be able to cope better with a country, the colonial powers prolonged a semi-colonial state for a few years by means of artificial federations, or by turning small islands, cities, sheikdoms and military bases into independent states or self-determining units after having 'consulted' the peoples concerned, the colonial powers and everybody else knowing that these units could never become nations since they lacked the most elementary conditions of a nation or of communal consciousness.

The great powers, then, whether immediately concerned or not, would support or oppose this or that newly formed state, and take a positive or negative stand in territorial disputes or other controversies according to their approval or disapproval of the government or political system of the new state. This so-called 'realpolitik' proved very short-sighted in the light of further developments, when overnight a coup or revolution would replace a pro-Western government with one sharply opposed to the West, or vice versa. Thus the immediate political advantages determining national borders or deciding whether a state should be formed later became utterly meaningless. The original governments lasted at best a few years, while the new state or its frontiers became fixed for decades if not centuries. So the new states were to bear the burden of an instability born of so much irrationality in their creation and in the making of their frontiers.

Once more it is worth speculating what would have happened if a healthy development had been secured for the newly independent colonial countries, especially those south of the Sahara: a settlement drawn up in accordance with the basic principles by the colonial powers and the liberated peoples in concert, with new political frontiers worked out with the same careful respect for national, ethnic and historical factors as was intended at the time of the transformation of Russia into the Soviet Union. A supra-national economic and semi-political organisation should have been provided as well, particularly in Africa. Naturally, all this would not have been a complete guarantee against revolutions and political upheavals, coups and dictatorships, but it could have been a safeguard against the outbreak of genocidal strife and civil wars in the new countries — wars to be fought with weapons provided by the more 'advanced' states. It would also have been a safeguard against the misuse of the sparse intelligentsia of these poverty-stricken countries in unrealistic attempts to achieve economic independence fostered by militant nationalism.

All in all, when we view the surprisingly fast and occasionally even smooth process of colonial liberation, we must conclude yet again that the results of half-hearted good deeds are depressingly similar to those of whole-hearted bad ones. The second triumphal march of self-determination appears as likely to fail as the first one. The partial contradictions, the built-in dissonance, provide the starting point for new crises. We may well expect another period of disillusionment which this time will attribute the troubles not to failures in applying the principle of self-determination, but to the principle itself. Already some portents of this can be seen and old criticisms of the principle can be heard again. Though there is no coherent theory attacking self-determination on a broad front – as fascism used to attack sovereignty of the people – we can hear a wide range of theoretical, practical and political arguments against the principle. It has been described as legally intangible, ambiguous, problematical and only partially applicable; it is said that at certain times and places its application can be difficult, even dangerous; it has been implied, without actually attacking the principle, that self-determination is in practice unnecessary and invalid. We must now briefly survey these arguments to see if the principle of self-determination could be becoming discredited in the same way as monarchic-feudal legitimacy.

The significance of the passage from monarchic-feudal legitimacy to democratic principles

If the principle of self-determination is still a valid basis for the international community, how far does this go back to the original meaning of that ideological and social change that replaced monarchic-feudal legitimacy with the principles of sovereignty of the people, human rights and self-determination?

This change meant more than the replacement of one possible basic governing principle by another; it meant more than establishing rule by the many – which is how the vacillations between monarchy, aristocracy and democracy were seen in antiquity. Until modern times it was generally thought that monarchy and aristocracy were better forms of government than rule by the many, which never became an enduring system in antiquity or in the Middle Ages, though it flourished for short periods. But more recently, with new democratic developments, the emphasis has been on deeper, more far-reaching change than rule of the many; it has been on the spread of a basic principle declaring equal human dignity and freedom for all men. Instead of a social order based on rule and its traditional prestige, democracy has involved change to another order based on objective achievement and service to the community. It has involved a significant advance towards rationality in the exercise of power, transforming power into a concept that is just, liberal, controlled, rational and unbiased, with a more profound respect for moral and human values.

The argument for aristocracy, which questioned the competence of the people to make vital decisions, is meaningless. Of course there is no guarantee of this. Monarchy and aristocracy did not imply that kings or barons were necessarily born good; merely that at certain times in history their position by birth was respected, as was the claim that their upbringing and social authority qualified them to perform certain duties. But in modern democracy with its convictions of sovereignty of the people and self-determination corresponding with human freedom and equal human dignity, birth is not accepted as a qualification. Also, these basic democratic principles, together with certain corresponding institutions (parliamentary government, institutionally established liberties limiting the exercise of power, the independence of the judiciary, etc.) have created a form of government that, if not the most comfortable, is certainly the most durable and humane so far devised.

All this shows that democracy makes increasing moral claims on government. Such claims, when made on monarchic-feudal legitimacy, were subordinated to the sense of submission to power, though with a quality of morality and freedom in the guise of loyalty, fidelity and the admitted duties of the sovereign. An evil ruler or overlord would be suffered in much the same way as the whims of the elements, until the situation became intolerable. But the free and common democratic consciousness, whether seen in the form of national self-determination, sovereignty of the people, or economic and administrative participation, is a far subtler phenomenon of mass psychology, for, rather than to persons, it relates to consciously held principles of social order and their symbols. When it detects contradiction between the principles, their symbols and reality, it reacts far more vehemently than did loyal subjects and serfs to wicked masters.

The lessons of the past two centuries show that political, social or economic systems which are not honestly justified by basic democratic principles and common consciousness provoke much more exacting and passionate ideological mass movements than were possible in earlier times. At best these explode in revolutions that straighten out the lies and contradictions by force; but when the revolution is delayed, or becomes discredited or diverted, then it grows into fatal and destructive waves of disillusion and political hysteria, which in an irrational and nihilistic way will often turn against an idealistic and moral concept of power and lead to catastrophic political fury and self-destruction.

In contrast to the past, when the abuse of power was accepted, the basic democratic principles of society are characterised by a frightening extremism directed not so much against the imperfection of the situation — mankind will always live in a state of imperfection — as against falsehoods and attitudes that are irreconcilable with the principles. In practical terms this means that mass movements based on reason and morality — the enforcement of freedom, equal human dignity, justice, sovereignty of the people and self-determination — are not mere expressions of pious desire, but are expressions of real, irresistible political necessity that must not be ignored. When surveying the various criticisms levelled against self-determination, one must keep in sight this almost unprecedented strength of the ideals forming the basis of democratic principles, and of the movements aimed at making them effective.

[5]

The Principle of
Self-Determination as a Spur to
Nationalism

Nation, fatherland and national consciousness

Critics of the concept of self-determination argue that it gives certain groups the right to become nations and establish national states – which fosters nationalism; and they argue that nationalism is anti-progressive, aggressive, oppressive and war-prone, and that it should be wholly suppressed for the progress of civilisation. This contrasts with the fact that the ideal of nationhood and the claim to national identity – springing from Western political ideas – are spreading all over the world. Liberation of the Third World is inevitably being realised through the creation of national states; but in some parts of the world it is evident that the problems and territorial conflicts of emerging nations will remain in dispute, and steps to prevent this, in whatever degree, call for means that are fundamentally opposed to the concept of freedom.

The relationship between the concepts of self-determination and nationhood and of democratic ideals of freedom imply the following equation: democratic freedom equals self-determination equals the nation state. On the other hand, nation state equals nationalism equals fascism and war. No doubt there must be grave errors to be found in both these equations.

Past and present meanings of the terms nation, fatherland, country, will be defined only so far as they are relevant to the argument. A nation is a social community larger than the earlier, more primitive communities; its aim is political in that it aspires to well-defined territory, organised so that national consciousness is shared by most if not all of the community. Common history, language and economic interests are often cited as criteria in the definition of a nation. But a historical background is not necessarily and in all cases a good framework; language has in many instances been a determining force – and with the increase of mass-communication its significance grows – but it is not always a decisive factor. An economic community of interests may strengthen a state, or the intention to form one, but this is not necessarily so – under certain circumstances, for instance with a favourable balance of power, communities with a weak or failing economy may survive as nations and states. It is not possible to give definite answers in deciding what are the desirable conditions or the right directions for nation-forming, or which of the conflicting aspirations are the right ones: whether a large, comprehensive unit is better than a smaller, more homogeneous one; whether historical claims are more desirable than ethnic or linguistic ones – in the dissolution of realms or colonial empires, it is not possible to determine whether the old, historic, administrative frontiers are more or less expedient than tribal, ethnic or linguistic borders. In a given case, the complex interrelationship of several factors will determine the actual way in which a nation may evolve. However, in specific situations it is possible for an objective and alert observer to predict the outcome.

Thus interpreted, a nation is not an absolute, everlasting phenomenon; nor is it a form of community that necessarily results from man's biological, psychological and social make-up. Many ages and empires have passed without their people having any conception of nationhood – though one should remember that they were largely under a continuous chain of despots and oligarchies, and power was regarded as a cosmic rather than a man-made creation; and the larger and more complex the unchecked political power, the less possible for a concept of nationhood to emerge. However, long before the revolutions of modern times there were communities with a public consciousness similar to present-day national consciousness. These were communities with considerable internal self-government and external independence, and their people were relatively active politically: for example, the city states of antiquity, tribal kingdoms, medieval cities and larger republics, peasant cantons and feudal kingdoms. So the relationship between the forming of relatively free political communities and the emergence of the concept of nation and fatherland is not entirely new. The great difference is that in these past 'nations' there was a narrower, aristocratic, semi-democratic concept of liberty and national consciousness confined to the elect and the privileged. It meant a common consciousness conflicting with various other loyalties and demands, such as those of the family, the clan, the tribe, the city, or religion – any of which could come to the fore to take precedence over national loyalty. As may be learnt from Plutarch, there was an elaborate ancient moral code supporting and fostering the sense of duty to one's country and calling for resistance and self-sacrifice for its own sake.

Nationhood as we conceive it today first appeared in the terminology of the French Revolution and other mass uprisings against monarchy and aristocracy. The first concepts of nationhood and national consciousness were not born at the time of the French Revolution, but they merged then into the modern ideal of liberty which proclaimed the equality and equal dignity of all men. These ideals became so widely accepted as to become an all-embracing mass phenomenon, unlike the former limited aristocratic, semi-democratic national sentiments. A new consciousness of common loyalty replaced the vacuum left by old loyalties to ruler and oligarchy, a concept symbolised by the nation based on the ideal of fatherland.

This means that this modern national consciousness, new in form, and aiming to dominate the political community, did have certain – though different – preliminary bonds of community. In fact, in the history of mankind ancient and vital forms of loyalty gradually merged into the single great stream of national consciousness: loyalties to the tribe or clan, the citizen's loyalties to his town or birthplace, loyalties to religious and military leaders, and those of the subject for his ruler, all formed its tributaries. The feelings for the homeland as they existed in the politically active, aristocratic and semi-democratic communities, feelings already discussed, became a natural part of the greater stream of national loyalty, simply by embracing the masses. Religious and social loyalties and those to political movements and parties contributed to the emergence of the nation state and national loyalty – as still happens today.

This diverse heritage, together with the way in which political consciousness has become democratised and popularised, welds the national consciousness of today into a frightening force; a force that is not likely to grow less in the near future. For the great majority of people in countries with modern mass opinion, and for many others, the strongest communal tie outside that of the family is to the nation, strong enough to evoke loyalty and self-sacrifice. They are feelings that exist regardless of power, social or political interests, of claims for domination or distorted ideologies, and they are not the result of them. Naturally such sociological aspects of nationhood and national consciousness do not justify an ideology based on nationalism, but as they are facts they cannot be dismissed by the repudiation of any such ideology.

The question, then, is: what are the causes of this dangerous aspect of nationalism – the dominating and aggressive elements – that came into being with communities based on political freedom, and in the context of national consciousness?

Positions of domination and submission among nations

The building and maintenance of a political framework, a political organisation, a 'state' is the main feature in the forming of national communities. Through this the nation and nation state have to become aware of the complexities, organisational and otherwise, that are typical of all communities, and especially the politically active ones. Problems, aims, plans, actions, successes and failures all become communal issues. Individuals feel a sense of loyalty and belonging to the community, a sense of solidarity with other members, that have both positive and negative sides. Identities and conflicts of interest may develop within the community; its existence may be threatened; it may be exposed to insults and injustices; it may have demands and claims against other communities, or vice versa. Problems of power may arise: power relationships may produce situations that entire national communities and their corresponding states have to face, differences in power bringing fears for survival, aggressive emotions, distinct feelings of inferiority or superiority, and above all the problem of domination and subjugation.

It is here that the essential difference lies between free nations, in the modern sense of the word, trying to form their states on the ideal of liberty and dignity for all, and those earlier nations not based on these principles – the slave-holding city states, tribal kingdoms, aristocratic republics and feudal kingdoms – which also proudly regarded themselves as free. For the nations of the past, force, oppression, wars of survival, conquests and brutal acts of revenge over insulted pride did not conflict in the least with patriotic and national feelings. A citizen of Athens, as a free citizen, could without qualm do with his slave as he pleased. For a German prince, the freedom of the German nation contained the right – *libertas Germanica* – for him to sell his subjects as soldiers to foreign princes. A Hungarian nobleman of the eighteenth century could feel bitter over lost Hungarian 'national freedom' when his emperor in Vienna tried to reduce the burdens of the Hungarian serfs. These communities, so jealously guarding their communal and individual liberties, challenged other, similar communities to chivalric battles, or wars of life and death, and conquered, annihilated, oppressed, punished or simply subjugated and absorbed their opponents, without any of these actions contradicting the fundamental principles of their aristocratic and, within limitations, democratic existence. But these actions are not acceptable to modern nations that protest against all forms of tyranny and proclaim equal freedom and dignity for all.

In this lies the most decisive problem in the formation of modern states, and in their inner tension. The state as the historical organ of power, domination and war, is shifting towards a social organisation based on free consent and agreement from one that has been based on dominance and aggression, so that certain forms of confrontation, primarily those based on domination and oppression, should cease in accordance with the Marxian dictum that 'no nation can be free whilst oppressing others'. But situations do arise where power relations, domination, war and fears for survival are apt to revive the temptations to use traditional means of dominance and force, even in free nations and states with the modern ideal of liberty. As previously mentioned, this can be seen in the development of European states in the nineteenth and twentieth centuries. There were instances when developed countries inherited slaves, conquests and colonies from their monarchic or aristocratic predecessors, or acquired them through their own ambitious militant politicians or enterprising citizens. Some nations found themselves facing minorities within their boundaries who had their own national consciousness and ambitions. In other cases, as a result of historic events, wars and subsequent peace settlements, nations became rulers over conquered territories with national minorities, or conflicts arose right at the start of a nation's formation concerning border territories with mixed populations. Or certain communities would dominate ones already existing, breeding hostility and competition for the leading role in forming the nation.

Modern democratic nations who are supposed to be establishing a society based on the ideals of liberty and equal dignity for all men should have solved, and still ought to solve these problems in accordance with the principles of liberty, equality before the law, respect for the sovereignty of the people and the principle of self-determination. On these grounds, all slavery and exploitation should have been abolished, conquered territories and colonies liberated; and disputes concerning the formation of states and nations, as well as other territorial and border problems, could have been solved by unbiased, objective methods. Nonetheless, the question as to how well a nation is able to comply with these requirements and how far it gives in to atavistic temptations of domination by force, depends on a complex interaction of many factors.

Factors prompting aggression and domination in the behaviour of nations

Amongst the factors leading to aggressive and dominating behaviour in nations, the level of progress reached in regard to the concept of liberty and the practical application of rights granted by liberty is the primary and most decisive factor in nations already formed and those in the process of formation. It is influenced by the nation's history and its political and social maturity. The interpretation and assessment of liberty by a nation covers a wide scale.

At one end of this scale are the nations that are most developed politically, with long-established traditions, formidable experience, and continuous practice of freedom. For them nation-forming is a process similar and parallel to that of a social organisation based on the principle of liberty and human dignity without discrimination. The basis is that a people evolves into a modern nation because of undergoing a process of democratisation and becoming conscious of its sovereignty within its borders; and despite all their dictatorial, imperialistic, exploiting, colonising interludes, this basis of modern nationhood has remained unharmed.

At the centre of the scale are those countries where patriotism and the demand for liberty comes from the narrower aristocratic, oligarchic, privileged or intellectual strata, trying to keep pace with the example of more developed countries, and not from the still comparatively passive masses, who are not mature enough to formulate or aspire towards national freedom. This was the case in Central and Eastern Europe at the turn of the eighteenth and nineteenth centuries, and it is still prevalent in various parts of the world today.

Finally, at the other end of the scale are those countries where the ruler himself is the initiator of movements to 'arouse national sentiments', while the masses are still totally passive. This is how European monarchs tried to arouse their people against Napoleon, and it is how rulers, wherever they exist in the Third World, are trying to do it today. The degree to which a ruler or oligarchy sees the superiority of developed countries in terms of power rather than greater liberty for the people, determines the character of their initiatives and how far the national consciousness becomes manifest in power, domination and militancy. Depending on this, national sentiments may be more restricted or may embrace all the wider aspects of freedom. This may explain why, in the last two hundred years throughout the world, the aspiration for nationhood has been spreading faster and more forcefully than that of reorganising society according to the principles of liberty and equality of human dignity. The two concepts appear to have become almost separated, although the existence of the former for any length of time is hard to conceive without the latter. Such paradoxical situations could never grow from spontaneous processes of evolving into a nation, and in any of the recent examples of national movements with a diminishing or even hostile attitude to freedom the ups and downs may end only when the nation finally joins the truly free ones at the upper end of the scale.

The degree of consciousness of freedom is not the only determining element in the temptation to display dominating and militant attitudes. Other contributing factors are the economic and power relationships which accompany efforts to realise concepts of freedom; the sacrifices demanded in giving up positions of power, economic interest and long-established territorial possessions; and ingrained feelings of superiority. Greatness of power and a reluctance to make sacrifices have induced even some of the developed and freedom-loving nations to oppress, dominate, absorb or annihilate far weaker and smaller communities; and, especially when there were racial, cultural or economic differences, it has not been difficult for the superior power to regard the doctrines of liberty as inapplicable, or to postpone applying them 'for the time being' — which in fact often meant for several generations. Frequently the apostles of freedom and humanitarianism arrived on the scene far too late. In the case of the the American War of Independence — an example to the whole world — it was possible simultaneously for it to reach victory while it was still considered the wrong time to abolish the gravest of human oppressions, negro slavery. Similarly, for more than a century after the proclamation of human rights, the most developed European countries could regard the domination of underdeveloped peoples through colonial rule as a natural relationship.

In the inevitable process of decolonisation the concepts of liberty should not be over- or underestimated; nor should the role of power and economic relations. Some state of power relations was necessary for the process to begin, but once established the ruling country's concept of liberty became decisive. This has already been shown in comparing the attitudes to decolonisation of the more developed Western countries with that of the Portuguese.

The experiences of national communities during their formation are also important: the political conflicts, insults, injustices and oppressions. For example, the revolutionary terror that irreparably damaged the outlook for liberty in France and the French Revolution's reputation throughout Europe was caused by reactionary forces attacking the Revolution; and in self-defence, this caused the revolutionary regime to develop into wars of conquest and a fight for survival, and became fearful of the collective frenzy of victories. These evoked opposing national sentiments and, with experiences of power, oppression, insults and war, united the national consciousness within the attacked and subjugated communities.

There are many other examples that show how, in the life of a community or nation, the more traumatic their experiences, the more they are inclined to seek security in intolerant and oppressive behaviour; and the less they have experienced injustice, humiliation, attack, oppression, war, threat of annihilation, the more they are willing to accept sacrifices for the ideals of freedom.

The forming of boundaries in evolving nations has also contributed to domination: neighbouring nations competing over border territories and vying for the loyalty of the populations concerned; or existing states, national units, federations and their members in conflict over which should be the protagonist in the formation of a nation. For example, from the beginning of the nineteenth century onwards there were three contestants as to which nation the Slovakian-speaking population should belong, living as it was in the Kingdom of Hungary under an Austrian emperor. (When someone praised the patriotism of one of his subjects, the Emperor Franz asked, with some embarrassment, 'Patriotism towards whom?') The Hapsburg realm wanted to modernise itself by becoming an Austrian nation, while inheriting the prestige and authority of the Holy Roman Empire which had been for many centuries associated with it. This might have been possible had it been a centralised state for as long as, say, France; but the Austrian efforts at centralisation were barely a hundred years old, while the title of the Austrian Empire was a creation of 1804. The Kingdom of Hungary, on the other hand, with its eight hundred years of history, and its strong awareness of a common destiny, wanted to create a Hungarian nation within its historic territory. This could have happened if the country had remained independent, had democratised itself at the appropriate time, and had not tried, like France, to make the country unilingual – which was done in an effort to regain independence and to prove the language competitive with German. The Slovaks, too, could have formed a nation, had they had an historically developed political framework, but they had none. They tried to compensate for this lack by spreading a sense of belonging to the great Slavonic family of nations, which they regarded as more formidable than the Austrian Empire and the Kingdom of Hungary, both in dispute over their claims for independent nationhood.

The three competing claims resulted in a long and complex struggle. At first, the Austrians got their way over the Hungarians and Slovaks; and then the Hungarian viewpoint was victorious over the Austrians and Slovaks; finally the Slovaks, with the help of the Czechs, triumphed over the Austrians and the Hungarians, but simultaneously developed a similiar struggle with the Czechs over the same problem. Further complications arose through numerous problems and disputes over the demarcation of authority. Both singly and collectively these problems gave ample opportunity for the national formations and movements to become imbued with a spirit that aspired to power and militancy.

It is these divergent factors that determine the extent of aggression and dominance in the process of nation-forming within the modern ideals of liberty. On the one hand we find nations with a serious concept of liberty and a relatively equal balance of power, confronting each other without suffering from the nightmares of annihilation, without notable border conflicts, settling their problems as stylishly as did Sweden and Norway, or Denmark and Iceland. On the other hand we see that political backwardness, an uneven balance of power, experiences breeding fear, a distorted collective mentality or complex territorial and border problems can magnify conflicts between nations almost to the point of genocide. All these more or less dangerous manifestations of aggression and dominance may be summarised under the term 'nationalism'. But nationalism cannot be regarded simply as an aggregate of actual manifestations, since it also represents a set of ideas, an ideology.

A digression on our contemporary political ideologies

Confrontation of political ideologies, with all the fanaticism of religious wars, is a characteristic of our age. Ideologies have been compared to religions, or secular substitutes for religions, by Raymond Aron, Arnold Toynbee, and others.

There are two common views of the nature of ideology: the first interprets it as a comprehensive, fully developed system of ideals, the second sees it as a substitute for ideals, or even as a system of false consciousness. In practice one ideology may be found to fit into the first category and another into the second; or it may be found that every ideology lies somewhere between these two extremes. But no ideology is a system of absolutely valid concepts, though each is related to some kind of valid, or once valid, concept. However, since an ideology not merely propagates concepts but also tries to realise and apply them involving strategies, tactics and politics – ideologies distort their concepts, and this is why the term ideology is so often pejorative. This belittling view is especially strong when ideologies are regarded as secular substitutes for religion. For the religious believer this makes them appear as cheap imitations of true religion; for the sceptic and anti-religious, it carries undertones of the worst expressions of religion – fanaticism, intolerance, the claim to prophetic clairvoyance and infallibility, dogmatism and persecution. But rather than make these analogies, we would do better to concentrate on the social content of ideologies.

The modern concept of liberty gives society heightened expectations and new goals, which may explain the vehemence and occasional intolerance of mass movements. The expectations, shared by intellectuals, the élite and the masses, project the vision of a free, equal, just and rational society based on common consent, with all forms of tyranny and exploitation abolished, with the sovereignty and self-determination of the people assured. In contemporary ideologies ways and means are suggested for realising these expectations and ideals, so that the concepts are thought of in terms of practical application – the means and weapons, strategies and tactics. Social, political and economic forces that impede progress are singled out and often accused of misrepresenting and abusing the concepts. In this general context, the long- and the short-term aims, the road to victory, are set up within the ideology. The stronger the sense of depredation and deception among the masses, the more vehement and intolerant the reverberations of the ideology become.

The distorting elements of power, dominance, militancy and self-interest are to be found as much in a movement following an ideology as they are in a nation, and they may simultaneously be the tools and the obstacles to the movement. The very concepts become political factors and political instruments. But if it is naive to think that a power that uses ideals in its vocabulary will also realise those ideals, it is cynical to claim that ideals are always mere slogans of power. Within the relationship between ideals and power there is a constant shifting of balance that determines which will be prime mover and which the instrument. To some degree all ideals, when they reach the stage of realisation, become affected by the distorting elements of power, dominance, force, militancy and self-interest: again and again new structures and organisations are overcome, expropriated and falsified by various manifestations of power, dominance and self-interest; again and again we find initially ascetic leaders becoming like potentates of the past, safeguarding and abusing their power in a similar way. Ideologies filled with promise fall under the suspicion that their function is merely to create, maintain and justify new types of power. And so a number of contradictory ideologies have developed, resulting from the sequence of disappointments in the move towards a society organised in accordance with the concepts of liberty and equal dignity for all men. With growing vehemence and intolerance, each tries to discredit the other. Disillusionment follows continual disappointments caused by ideologies getting caught in the traps of power and force; and rational criticism of their contradictions and lack of realism proves futile.

If we were able to stand back from the situation, we would be aware of the impressive progress that has taken place in the techniques that can humanise, rationalise and create a social order based on human consent – impressive when compared with the modest claims of the past when brutal repression was taken for granted. But, as things are, such progress moves through cycles of intensified expectations, betrayed hopes and repeated gestures of revision and improvement, and struggles rage between different ideologies and the masses grow more impatient, so that is is often difficult to recognise what has been achieved.

According to Toynbee, the predominant ideologies of our time – the secular substitutes for religion – are individualism, communism and nationalism. He points out that whenever these three find themselves in friction, the most dangerous among them – nationalism – invariably triumphs.

These three categories for contemporary ideologies, each in its way related to the concept of liberty, seem convincing, but individualism is not a completely satisfactory term for a complex which is variously called liberalism, bourgeois democracy, capitalist ideology or 'the American way of life'; while the category of communism should be extended to include other types of socialism whether more inclined to compromise or to dogmatism.

We can probably add another category: there still exists an authoritarian-aristocratic principle which, although defensive in its nature, may be considered an ideology. In the past it was dominant in Europe and had universal validity, and although it has now vanished in essence many of its aspects linger stubbornly on. Occasionally it appears under the old-style mantle of the Holy Alliance as an undisguised reactionary force, but generally it assumes more modern forms. However, it no longer commands the support of the masses except when it finds a common platform with nationalism: fascism, containing a distorted kind of nationalism, incorporated certain shreds of this authoritarian-aristocratic view after it had been stripped of its validity – its original, tradition-guarding, aristocratic content.

What is the place of nationalism among these contemporary ideologies? What we have said about ideologies in general – their distortion by elements of power or force – holds good for individualism-liberalism and for socialism-communism. And we should observe that these two ideologies both represent serious socio-economic systems and are comprehensive ideological structures in their own rights. Both sprang from the concept of liberty, from the ideal of equal freedom and dignity for all. Both received their convictions from these concepts – although each may have different, narrower interpretations of these great ideals and they seem to be almost diametrically opposed to one another. While running the risk of making a sweeping generalisation, one may say that individualism-idealism primarily and almost exclusively emphasises the concept of freedom, with stress on freedom of economy and enterprise, while socialism-communism emphasises equality, social justice and abolition of economic exploitation. Here we may criticise them both in that they treat certain partial aspects of liberty and equal human dignity as if these represented the whole concept and thus they split the concept of freedom into two separate spheres of liberalism and socialism. We may also criticise them because, their chief protagonists being the superpowers of the world, they have become contaminated by dangerous elements of the desire to rule, and by Machiavellian techniques. Yet again we may criticise them on the ground that, as a result of this contamination, they equate programmes of principles and concepts with class interests and political actions – programmes for practical action become handicapped by ideological prejudices and unrealities, while principles often become corrupted and falsified by short-term tactics. It could be said that one fears the excessive power of the state and, while proclaiming the cause of liberty, arrives at a justification for economic exploitation, whereas the other, fearing this exploitation, creates a system in which people are exposed to domination by bureaucracy. Both have had disastrous consequences in the past and may have them again. But the fact remains that neither individualism-liberalism nor socialism-communism has turned against the democratic concept of liberty from which it originally developed. Whatever the symptoms that show from time to time under the demoralising influence of power, war and self-interest, and regardless of their rigidity and dogmatism, both ideologies maintain an inner force capable of efforts for improvement and purification, and have liberty as their standard; both ideologies maintain programmes with serious claim to universal validity, and both are capable of functioning at given places and times. They maintain contact with the significant currents of human thought, and they maintain their ability to suggest universal validity and to argue this, whether or not they are in power: in fact these potentials are often the stronger if the ideology in question is not in a dominant position.

Nationalism and patriotism

Is it possible to say that nationalism has also kept a programme in keeping with the concept of liberty – despite deviations? Is it able to function on a world-wide scale? Has it universal validity and serious conceptual weight?

Nationalism is also referred to as nationalistic behaviour or nationalistic ideology. Generally speaking, the term is applied to different concepts which are related but not identical. For some it means plain national sentiments, national consciousness; for others a stronger, more vehement show of feelings. Nationalism is often identified with efforts towards independence, and with the establishment of nation states, but even more often it is interpreted as efforts in the national interest using forceful means. It is also frequently associated with the aggressive domination that develops from political backwardness, uneven power relations and oppression, and from the complex problems of survival and frontier delineation. Finally, the terms nationalist and nationalism also mean an attitude, a concept, a sort of ideology in which the nation forms the pivot of the system.

These interpretations have a common feature: they all have a pejorative, derogatory element. We normally tend to speak of nationalism as a dangerous, harmful and distorted ideology, and we condemn the aggressive and domineering qualities. When efforts for national interests are narrow-minded and petty, or when they are considered to be harmful, liable to lead to conflict, unjustified and extreme, we call it nationalism. Thus, a large political unit regards a smaller unit's aspirations for independence as a kind of nationalism that has grown from a narrow-minded, pettifogging spirit of separatism, while the smaller units see efforts for unification as aggressive nationalism, derived from imperialism and the wish to dominate. The one who is 'right' is always determined by which of the claims is in 'true harmony' with the nation-forming trend and which tries to impede this. Similarly, it is called nationalism when the simplest, most natural display of national sentiment and consciousness is in contradiction with an internationalist concept or another nationalistic prejudice; and this is why nations in conflict with one another often regard their own national loyalty and solidarity as natural, spontaneous, healthy, while the national consciousness of their opponent is artificially fostered, harmful, and stirred up by wicked agitators. On the other hand, those who willingly accept the label of nationalism do so either to display their identification with its aggressive-domineering elements, or in defiance of the charges against them; and nations that are accused of narrow-minded nationalism when their claims are justified will accept the label ostentatiously, being well aware that it is a pejorative one.

So the derogatory and pejorative associations of the terms nationalism and nationalistic should be taken into account, nationalism meaning the aggression and domination of a nationalistic mentality with its distorted concept in regard to the nation. But these terms should not be used when referring to manifestations of national sentiments and consciousness of a community, or to the efforts to establish national states. Here it is reasonable to distinguish between patriotism, meaning the natural, cohesive elements of national consciousness, and the harmful, aggressive elements of nationalism. Patriotism has become the more appropriate term for a healthy national consciousness, while nationalism, with its harmful associations, refers to problems more associated with territory than with people. (It is paradoxical that the word patriotism derives from one with territorial connotations – the Latin *patria,* fatherland – while nationalism derives from one concerned with birth, individuals, people.)

Just as liberal individualism is an ideology primarily of freedom, and socialism-communism one primarily of equality and social justice, so patriotism and nationalism are ideologies primarily of the nation. But whereas systems may be needed to further the concepts of liberty, equality and social justice, all that is needed for the concepts of nation and national consciousness is the assertion that they are based on the right to freedom and equal human dignity, and that the causes of the community are everyone's causes; and accordingly members of the community as a whole have the right to decide its political and social systems, the national and territorial framework. This is equivalent to the general democratic concept of liberty, and the principle of sovereignty of the people and the right to self-determination.

Neither does the formation of a nation state need an ideology. The nation state develops from the will and self-determination of the people to develop a nation state rather than to form political organisations on a higher, supra-national level. Similarly, there is no ideology represented when an individual with an emotionally intense national consciousness, loyalty and solidarity calls himself a nationalist, any more than there is an ideology of 'familyism' for one who loves his parents or 'urbanism' for one who loves his native town.

However, when a nation state occurs through the break-up or unification of previous units rather than through an inherited framework of territory and population, in order to justify its existence it then seems to need a programme with many of the features of an ideology. There is need for a strong assertion of the necessity of national sovereignty, national unification, more than is customary among stable and well-established nations. Such a programme usually calls for a fostering of characteristic national features, and for acceptance of patriotic sacrifices in the aim for independence or unification – sacrifices which do not necessarily involve aggressive-domineering tendencies.

Patriotism, then, is much closer to the concept of liberty than to that of nationalism; but in spite – or perhaps because – of this, it forms an ideology of much simpler and less defined concepts. Although concepts are in general against aggression, nationalism contains more ideological concepts than patriotism with its rather sublime ideals.

Nationalism as an aggressive attitude and as an ideology

Nations developed a system of ideals as a means of justifying aggression and domination when, historically, aggression ceased to be the normal way of conducting policies and had to be reconciled with ideals of liberty. For thousands of years aggression and domination were regarded as normal, without any need for justification. Autocracies and oligarchies were conditioned to fight and conquer, as we have seen, though ancient republics and principalities did have some concept of free democratic nationhood, it was in no way associated with a specifically nationalistic system of ideas − rather it was based on primitive and flattering aristocratic legends of the nation's origin, with heroic and moralising tales fostering national pride and conquest.

The development of concepts justifying aggression and domination may be observed among nation states established on the modern principles of liberty. This happens when nations are provoked to show aggression and domination because of political factors, power structures, traumatic experiences, problems of survival or delineation of frontiers leading to political objectives that are out of tune with the democratic concept of nationhood. As these nations are unwilling to give up the concept of liberty, a tension develops between the concept and those militant, domineering features that are an essential part of their existence. This is why the domineering-militant attitude needs explanations on a conceptual level: it has to be reconciled with the ideals of liberty, and those ideals have to be complemented by theories and programmes for militant domination.

Such were 'the white man's burden', justifying his colonial rule, and the spreading of the democratic ideals of the French Revolution in order to justify the French military conquests in Europe. Various forms of 'pan-isms', historic claims or the safeguarding of historical possessions may also fall into this category, as may the 'mission' of certain dynasties and aristocracies, the 'special aptitude for nation-forming', and the cultural or racial 'superiority' or 'democratic virtues' of certain nations.

The degree to which these justifications − varying in validity − have penetrated a nation's life has determined the extent to which autocratic-oligarchic concepts have been revived. The greater the process of penetration, the more the nation has moved against the opponents of its own distorted national concept − primarily against other nations, not against the antiquated monarchic-aristocratic institutions which lost their *raison d'être* and were even, on occasion, given certain privileges if they identified themselves with the national cause, either because of fear or a wish to dominate.

In the most extreme cases, the theoretical justifications of aggression and dominance have reached the point of complete dismissal of the concepts of liberty, and open acceptance of the aristocratic-oligarchic viewpoints aimed at exploitation. This has been most apt to happen among, nations or other groups of people who, in the name of liberty, have been exposed to collective insults, threats to survival and mass humiliation – blows that are particularly dangerous if suffered by nations or nation-like groups who were formerly contaminated by the spirit of domination and lost their power in humiliating circumstances. It happened to the Southerners in the United States after the Civil War, to the Germans after Versailles and to the French settlers who had to leave Algeria.

Equally grave are the pathological fears that may result from such situations, fears of their recurrence and even more of total annihilation. These are the fears of the South African white man and of the Southern whites in the United States who, after the Civil War, gradually regained some of their former dominance. And from such fears spring political demands that provoke the very dangers, humiliations and annihilation they seek to avoid.

Finally, there are the distortions and conflicts that attack the ideal of liberty when a strong nation, claiming to be free, keeps a weaker one oppressed and humilated. Such conditions allow the growth of ideas that go further than mere self-deception and transparent untruth – monstrous concepts such as fascism, racism, racial persecution, cults of personality and violence, the Black Muslim Movement, etc., representing a senseless fear, disillusionment or hatred of liberty, even the total madness of the tyrant, with the force of a mass movement. These pathological phenomena are not, of course, permanent, though their effectiveness is related to the degree of humiliation suffered – and they can become mass issues.

So we may say that there is irreconcilable contradiction in all such aggressive-domineering ideologies, or pseudo-ideologies: they cannot be both for and against freedom, and to suggest any compatibility with the concept of liberty is sheer nonsense. And the contradictions are more encompassing than this. Extreme movements still claim mass support, which is the motive force of national movements for freedom, and they expect to develop the characteristics of the free man – spontaneity, enthusiasm, responsibility in action and conscious self-sacrifice – with allowing the community the basic needs of the free man.

These contradictions have produced grave consequences. For example, the Southern plantation-owner could say, 'I, as a free citizen of the United States, can do with my negroes as I please', while under a constitution that proclaimed human rights and equality for all. And other landowners and capitalists have understood their own freedom in terms of the subjugation of others; while the 'white man' only emphasised his 'burden' when it ceased to be advantageous to him. Yet again, the French tried extending their territory in the name of spreading the ideals of the French

Revolution. And public life in Hungary before the First World War was equally absurd and contradictory, as in other countries with national minorities: all citizens were equal members of the state, but those who adopted the state language and tried to enforce it on others were the better patriots.

Such examples show that, in most cases national policies and movements that falsify or reject the concept of liberty eventually pay a high price for this through spectacular failure, compromise or corruption of democracy — though occasionally sheer force combined with luck may bring success to such policies.

After this, it is difficult to think that nationalism could develop a cohesive system of thought that could be called an ideology. If we were to accept it as an ideology would mean giving too much weight to fragmentary concepts and pseudo-ideas that show a surface relationship originating from misleading situations, but without any common basis of ideals or concepts. Despite the fact that there are plenty of precedents for their actions, nationalist 'teachings' have glorified dominance, racial superiority, war and conquest. But, for the reasons shown, they have few antecedents among important modern concepts. Nietzsche is the only nationalist thinker of any significance — with his controversial and clearly dangerous ideas. But he preferred his own aristocratic viewpoint with its claims to universal validity to the half-baked concepts of the national movements of his day, for which he showed some contempt. The national concepts incorporated only fragments of the aristocratic-authoritarian principle and deprived it of its claim to universality by using it in the interests of one nation against another.

This means that there is no nationalism as such, only nationalisms, which in effect cancel each other out by each claiming to be the ethnically superior. Ideas range from the exaggerated glorification of political and cultural accomplishments of vanished empires and of suppressed races, to theories of racial supremacy, claims to domination, even world domination; they range from touching naivete and outright stupidity to the horror of mass murder. So the 'concepts' of various nationalisms have not survived their practical manifestations.

There are still three ideologies that share the ideal of liberty: liberalism, socialism and — with the least conceptual content — patriotism. Nationalism, if we are still to apply this term to aggressive and domineering attitudes and fragmentary concepts, is a deformed product.

The relationship between nationalism, nation and self-determination

Toynbee's contention — that whenever the three contemporary ideologies, individualism, communision and nationalism, have been in conflict, nationalism has triumphed — is open to differing interpretations; it is a kind of half-truth.

We could argue that twenty-odd years ago individualism and communism combined to overcome the most destructive nationalism of the age. Or that nationalism is increasing in strength and conflict. But Tonybee was referring to the growing characteristics of nationalism in the two superpowers rather than the turmoils of smaller nations, and this holds some validity. However, in the struggle between ideologies it is not proved that nationalism is the overriding force. The truth in Toynbee's theory is that the nation, as a category, has proved itself stronger than other cohesive factors within a community. But nationalisms, as ideologies, have never triumphed on any battlefield, either conceptual or practical.

A state with the ideology of either individualism-liberalism or socialism-communism continues to be a nation, its organisation remains a state and its territories the fatherland. So everything that has been said about the nation, fatherland, national consciousness, nation state and nationalism applies to them too. As with other nations, if they should feel they must justify their position and actions in any conceptual way, then these concepts assume the misconceptions of nationalism, even though they may be called distortions of individualism-liberalism or socialism-communism. Here nationalism has not 'triumphed' as a system of thought and programme, or as a secular substitute for religion, over the other two ideologies; rather the nation as a communal reality has proved itself stronger than either of the ideologies and their social programmes, power and interests.

A consciousness of being tied to a social group, a place, history – i.e. a nation – was a social reality long before awareness of personal and political freedom, or equal human dignity and social justice, which are now important elements of both liberalism and socialism. Individualism-liberalism and socialism-communism and the concepts of modern nationhood all spring from the central idea of democratic liberty. But it is the ideology of the nation, patriotism, with the least dependence on concepts that carries the greatest weight.

Contrary to Toynbee's thesis, whenever the principle of self-determination – the only valid principle of free nationhood – is used against nationalism, the so-called concepts of nationalism simply melt away. So it was with the 'white man's burden', the racial 'superiority' of the Northern races or the 'cohesive' power of St Stephen's crown. In a similar way we should observe that the contradictions between the programmes of freedom and of equality melt away when faced with a concept of liberty that is not influenced by economic and power interests. Now we may find the errors in the equations that lead from freedom and self-determination to the most destructive forms of nationalism.

Various nationalisms and other symptoms of crisis are components in the transition from the first ideals of liberty to its actual realisation in a functioning social structure – and we are still in this transitional period. The nation state only follows the principle of self-determination at certain points of development, and nationalisms grow wherever it breaks with the self-determination principle, based as it is on the concept of liberty. So self-determination is not the cause of nationalism. Rather it is the only real remedy against domination, subjugation and the fear from which nationalisms spring. It is the selfsame principle of self-determination that can both inspire nation states and solve their conflicts – providing it is consistently applied. So the concept of liberty needs to be taken literally, without any distortions; it needs to be embodied in a new type of state, society and international community of states, permeating the whole. Unless this happens, extremes of tension develop amongst intellectuals, the élite, the masses, to the extent that they are uncontrollable by traditional methods of exercising power.

[6]

The Principle of Self-Determination as an Impediment to International Integration

The programmes of a world-wide central power and of the domination of an élite

There is an important argument used against self-determination, and it is connected with the first argument condemning nationalism. It is that self-determination, having enabled nation states to grow, causes the community of states to drift towards fragmentation or 'Balkanisation'. In this way it impedes the evolution of higher forms of integration — federations, continental or subcontinental units, even a world state — which follows the current trends towards unity and world-wide technical progress.

According to this argument, the need for such comprehensive units is far more important than individual national self-determination. The will for self-determination does not aim at integration of units, even though it is able to, and if it does not recognise this as an evolutionary need then integration must be imposed on the masses who are unable to see their own best interests. It is pointed out that in global integration our political and social progress has fallen way behind scientific progress, especially in mass destruction — so global integration cannot wait for the common will. A central global power is the only solution to avert the threatening nightmares of self-destruction and famine, the only way to lead the largely passive masses to peace and prosperity. All else, freedom, equality, sovereignty of the people, self-determination or nation state, are simply irrelevant for none can save mankind from annihilation.

But opinions differ as to how this is to be achieved. Some think that a world state is required — and possible, since peace-keeping empires have managed in the past with less sophisticated instruments. The world state could be in the form of either a centralised world dictatorship or a federal formation with a strong central power. The advocates of this solution seldom clarify the relationship of this would-be organisation with today's great powers, particularly the superpowers. Some would appoint one or other of the superpowers, according to preference, to have such overwhelming world hegemony as to force all the other states to stop warring among themselves. There are those who would retain the present multitude of states while giving the right to solve the most burning problems – especially war and famine – to a supreme organisation with the ability to coerce. This suggestion in practice prescribes a world government with well-defined powers, and a global world police force stronger than any existing national army.

It would be gross irresponsibility to make light of the dangers in these suggestions, and even worse to consider the use of man's suicidal weapons as permissible for any purpose whatsoever. And it would show total lack of imagination to dismiss these ideas out of hand as improbable or unfeasible. History is too rich in possible permutations to allow us to declare anything impossible merely because it is hard to envisage. Events have shown that possibilities seen at first as daydreams have become realities much faster than even their exponents foresaw. If one makes an apparently none-too-feasible solution appear the only solution this could, through disappointments and disillusionment, hasten the very fate the solution was meant to avert. For all the apparent loftiness and generosity of the idea of world government, in an actual situation it may prove to be just as irresponsible and lacking in imagination as opposition to the idea on the grounds of impracticality.

Those who see our only salvation in the speedy formation of a central power with global authority should ponder the conditions of creating and maintaining such a power. The speedy creation of such a power centre, regardless of the will of nations, could only come through war and conquest or through an overwhelming superiority of force. This lesson of past experience still applies to our present stage of social evolution. But war and conquest must for the present be rejected, for these would probably cause a situation in which a central global authority was created by the very catastrophe it was designed to avert. And the formation of a central power through an existing global superiority of force shows no more promise, since there are several nuclear powers in existence.

But let us use our imagination. Let us suppose that a combination of unforeseen developments brings about such a one-sided superiority of power. This is not enough for the creation of a central global power. For this it is important that the leaders of all countries concerned, together with world public opinion and common consciousness, should show clear-sightedness, courage, fairness and restraint. In view of the psychotically distorted image of their opponents' political systems that is held by the leaders and public of the present major powers, combined with their amazing inability to understand each other's political language, we can expect the same horrifying consequences from the emergence of a one-sided superiority of power as from a pre-emptive war.

But if such a central global power should evolve through peaceful means, it would need to be maintained – and the instruments of power are notoriously unreliable. So the conditions for its continuous, universal, effective and objective functioning would have to be created and maintained. The first need would be for an administrative apparatus with a public spirit and sense of duty, and, within this, a loyal, powerful and effective world police force. The magnitude of the problems that the construction of such an apparatus and police force presents, let alone securing their public spirit, efficiency and loyalty, will be appreciated by all who have seen how difficult it is for existing world organisations to rely on their staff against the pull of national loyalties. This problem would be particularly critical when a world police force might have to act with resolution against local opposition; and it could never in any way succumb to the temptation of participating in any rivalry for world power, let alone in a global civil war. A long process of indoctrination and forming of tradition must precede the emergence of a decent army, ever ready to obey the civil authorities; and such a sensitive instrument is easily corrupted. But if all this cannot be evolved speedily for a world government, then such a global power would be just another, supremely dangerous potential centre of coercion – with threat of conflict and disintegration. And then there is likely to be rivalry for the possession of such a power centre, with results no different from the familiar phenomena of international tension and war. And there might even be no safeguard against global nuclear war.

Keeping these dangers in mind, there is the possibility that a world civil service and police force of the necessary loyalty and public spirit could be achieved through the ascent to power of a global élite, seen by some as one of professional-technical-economic experts, by others as an ideological or political élite. There has been a tendency towards the growth of élites in many forms and within many kinds of national and state frameworks, so it would be merely an extension of this to global proportions.

In fact, in the course of the social transition from domination by an élite with the prestige of birth and wealth to one based on performance, an élite of men with a high level of objective performance is evolving. This is taking place all over the world in political, administrative and economic fields. But the evolution of a meritocracy is entangled with the rearguard action of the former élite of birth and wealth which, having lost its function and prestige, defends its position by basing its claims on more contemporary premises. The evolution of a meritocracy is also up against political and ideological movements – so the formation of an élite is handicapped by a variety of claims to power and rule. But real meritocracy is characterised precisely by the absence of a claim to dominance, and the value of its performance should speak for itself, to stronger effect than it did for the former privileged classes.

We are not going to discuss all the ideological, political and economic differences which would have to be resolved before a global élite could develop — which is hardly possible in the near future. But we must mention one prerequisite to any programme for creating a central global power: such a power, such a rule by a world élite, could only function if there were to be universal agreement over the rules and procedures the leaders and supreme organisations would follow. These would have to cover the ways and means whereby a world government could ascend to power, the way in which it would exercise its power, determining who could be a member of the global élite. In other words, even in the case of a world state and élite, there is still the problem of the legitimacy of power as the one possible source of loyalty on the part of both functionaries and subjects.

Possible sources of the legitimacy of a world-wide central power and of the domination of an élite

Ultimately, the source of legitimacy, the legality of power, lies in the common conviction that accepts it. This is so even with monarchic or aristocratic power. If such a power is to possess stability it must be supported by common conviction, even though there is no institutional participation in public affairs by the masses: in effect, through their very passivity, the masses delegate to the central power the right to conduct public affairs.

For a central global power ruled by an élite, it is not enough to formulate correct programmes. One must ask if there exists, or will exist in the foreseeable future, a common conviction that feels obliged to obey the central power and follow the élite. It has been suggested that under the conditions of modern mass communication and techniques, public opinion and common conviction can be technically operated, manipulated at will, so that control lies with the authorities — who are also favoured by symptoms of increasing passivity among the masses. Even in countries with a long democratic tradition it appears that the masses are weary of politics, which seem to have become more and more involved; while in less advanced countries they have never acquired the habit of influencing politics. Because the institutions of a formal democracy are, in fact, manipulated from above, the masses have become apathetic; they want, not democracy and politics in general, but simply peace and prosperity with a strong government to provide security and an effective élite.

There is a lot of truth in this analysis. Yet it completely misconstrues the true communal and psychological state of the masses. However passive they may on occasion seem, the masses today would not consent to restrictions of their individual and communal influence, even if there were to be a simultaneous improvement in their material situation. They value their active participation in affairs and their own opinions, and would object to attempts to manipulate them, or claims to rule by a central power. The situation today is quite different from when the great peace-keeping empires were dealing with obedient masses of people who did not know the 'poison' of freedom and nationalism. It is true that even the most politically advanced masses get tired of the over-advertised forms of politics, and that they continue to want a strong administration capable of maintaining law and order, and an efficient élite — but only provided it is efficient and that it is not a privileged group disguising domination as efficiency. As it is, the growing political consciousness of today's masses is unprecedented in history, and it is demanding increasingly exacting standards of liberty, equality, justice, prosperity, legality and truth. The people do not expect to give constant advice to those in power, or to organise direct power through mass movements of daily plebiscites, but they do expect to participate in the decisions of authority and have their share of material goods, as dictated by common conviction and the sense of justice; and they do expect to be allowed to choose the social and governmental forms under which they wish to live and to be able to trust them — or failing that to be able to alter them; and they expect to be directed by an élite whose achievements command public respect, without any claim to domination; and, if occasion should arise, they expect that each nation should be allowed to make its own decisions over the formation of the state or its relationship to another state.

The peoples of the world do not give up these claims, even though they may sometimes appear to be gullible and bored with certain aspects of politics — and it is not easy to mislead them for long. The people of the Third World, too, are growing less passive as they emerge from their poverty and backwardness.

There has been hardly a government since the time of Hitler that has dared to deny the existence of the democratic demands of the masses. Even contemporary autocracies tend to recognise the demands of the public and recognise the hopelessness of trying to manipulate them out of existence by means of mass communications. In general they feel it necessary to show themselves able to activate democratic demand in some way, however distorted, such as stirring up aggressive nationalism. But such people, forced to live within this freakish or manipulated public framework, are not the same as the obedient, passive peoples of bygone empires. As we have shown, they react to the shortcomings and falsehoods with revolutionary movements, political hysteria or seething discontent. Every power, including any possible global authority, is faced with this, and if they do not have the active political approval of the masses their own behaviour and perceptions will be affected. Experience shows that a strong link between those in power and the common will is essential, and it is dangerous for a government to feel itself able and entitled to lead the passive, ignorant masses on the road to happiness without their consent. There are frightening examples that show how the most competent, sincere and incorruptible government and élite can, in a surprisingly short time, become senselessly tyrannical, cynically disillusioned and shamelessly corrupt.

Therefore, we have reason to suspect that the programmes for a world dictatorship and rule by élite, for all their ostensible progressiveness, are not representative of the future but are in many ways a superficial modern version of the dominance-oriented principles of monarchism and aristocratism – just like the similar elements of nationalistic ideologies.

Though these ideas of a world state or world élite may appear utopian and impractical, we do not really have the necessary historical perspective to judge them. The chief trouble with these ideas is that in turning the alternatives of a world state or a multitude of states, and élite rule or mass rule, into the decisive elements, they lay the main emphasis on the forms of power, rule, and their extent and application, rather than on the social and psychological conditions of their functioning. Today's advanced technology and communication would, indeed, make it possible for a single authority to administer a world state, which helps this kind of thinking. But there is more involved than administrative techniques.

Toynbee's thoughts on the ambitions of ancient cultures to create a world state may be inspiring, but there can be an over-evaluation of large centralised states compared to a well-balanced multitude of states. The real organisational peaks of past cultures occurred not when the great states claimed world dominance, but when there were great legitimacies of global extent, whether they were attached to unified states or to groups of states. With the primitive administrative instruments of the sixth century B.C. it was already possible for there to be a world empire stretching from the Aegean Sea to India, but resistance was still shown to the Persian Empire by the group of Greek city states, each hardly larger than a village of today. The Greek city states left a legacy of political achievements no less than those of the Persian Empire, even though they later destroyed themselves in suicidal wars and had to submit to newer world empires, which in turn tore themselves apart in century-long civil wars. Size or strength of power did not bring respite to the series of catastrophes; only political systems that could create a stable form of legitimacy brought this, whether it was in the form of empires such as the Roman Empire, or multitudes of states, as in Europe of the seventeenth and eighteenth centuries, or monarchies, aristocracies or democracies. And in our own day it seems clear that there is no other valid form of legitimacy than that which rests upon sovereignty of the people and self-determination.

The needless contradiction between self-determination and higher integration, and a gradual approach to higher integration

For all that has been said, and even with the dismembered situation of mankind and the present strength of the concept of the nation state, there is still truth in the argument that the higher forms of integration, including some global integration, are already conceivable. Such is a foreseeable development and a fairly urgent need. But there is no reason to regard this idea as opposed to the principle of self-determination.

When at the time of the French Revolution, and later the Russian Revolution, the public tried taking over the political framework, there seemed to be an opportunity for fraternal alliance and for a universal political consciousness — indeed it seemed a natural extension. Time has shown that the process would be neither simple nor fast. National community consciousness has grown with more speed than the functioning of the principle and institutions of freedom, which were meant to run parallel.

This does not mean that the nation state is the chief obstacle to integration, or that there is any need for a battle against claims to separate national identity. It is fruitless to place the interests of mankind beside that of one nation. As a matter of principle mankind's interests must be paramount. But it is much easier to define the interests of a nation than those of all mankind, which is still too remote a unit for the common consciousness. The nation seems to be the largest political community with which the majority of people today are able to communicate without difficulty. Beyond the limits of the nation people feel foreign. The framework of the nation and its state provide the conditions for successful communal activity, within the comprehension of the people. This is so regardless of size: it applies to small and great, and even to irrationally formed national communities, and it is independent of any ideology. This is the state of affairs today between the nation and the nation state on the one hand and higher forms of integration on the other.

Thus self-determination does not block the way to greater integration. Whether it produces nation states or a world state depends on the disposition of the people. But as it is applied today, at the present stage of the development of common consciousness, self-determination is directed mostly at the formation of nation states, with only modest attempts at supra-national and even less at global integration.

Yet optimism is not out of place — for when the opportunities allow, the principle of freedom works against the forces that turn nations against each other. The growth of integration needs the support of outward stability and inner freedom in a nation, as can be seen in comparing the more advanced countries with those recently liberated. The limited amount of progress is partly due to the self-interest or the despair of individual nations, but also to the indifference or impotence of the great powers and international organisations. The often painful process of nation-formation needs, therefore, to be made smoother and easier, with greater help for existing new nations to reach the stage of fulfilment and security. Help is needed to liquidate the power interests, claims to aggressive impulses and nationalistic ideologies that have been polluting national consciousness and interests, which would in turn help to create harmony between national interests and higher integration. And it would be more effective than the unpromising struggle against national consciousness and national interests.

The national framework needs to be built upon rather than destroyed. And the road to integration probably leads indirectly to a world state through political formations which contain continents or subcontinents, great common political undertakings or cultural entities. These, if only because of their size and coherent purposes, are closer to the cause of mankind than are the nation states. And there are signs today that show, in the self-determining will of the peoples, a groping towards a measure of loosely constructed global integration.

Once a higher form of integration is strengthened, it is typical for it to assume certain aspects of a nation or fatherland, either peaceful aspects or, perhaps, fights arising between individual nations and fatherlands within its borders.

The Soviet Union consists of individually aware nations, but its populations consider the whole as a fatherland. When Western European integration began, a debate started as to whether a super-fatherland should be allowed to supersede the individual fatherlands.

Unfortunately there is reason to assume that, once the whole of mankind constitutes one large integrated unit, the higher form will lose its somewhat vague benevolent aspect and adopt the behaviour of a community with wills, demands and claims, with the danger of domineering, power-oriented and aggressive ideologies, just like any other human community organised for action.

Self-determination and federation

The principles of self-determination and of federation as a form of higher integration are both related to the ideal of freedom, but they are often seen as opposing one another.

A federation may be created voluntarily by separate entities, or it may be created by an existing state structure in order to secure greater autonomy and self-determination for its component parts. Or, in the face of a centralising trend, it may involve the maintenance of the autonomy of the members of an existing federation. In recent times there has been a shift of emphasis towards the view that federations must be formed and maintained, and that they must be protected from separatist tendencies. The argument behind this view is that, through federation, larger, more viable units can be formed, which are more suitable for further integration. Freedom is not an issue, and the very freedom which exists within a federation is thus degraded to become a means to an end that will aid its members' appetite for integration. In this view, every federation that enlarges the framework of a state is commendable; and every tendency against federation is harmful to the cause of integration.

This confuses concept with objective. The intrinsic value of federation can only be determined by the freedoms within it: by the degree of freedom, justice, self-determination and coexistence; by the amount of agreement — common will, resolution to from a nation or supra-national structure, homogeneity, common basic principles, intentions and interests that make it a cohesive force. The measure of this agreement shows how far the trends towards growth or disintegration of the federation coincide with the actual trends towards nation-formation, supra-national integration or super-nation formation.

The principle of federation has no value in itself. Its value is derived from the principle of freedom, it is not itself a standard for other values. It is not possible to approve every trend towards federalisation. Nor can we say that the federalisation of existing units or the appearance of new federations is in itself progressive or retrograde. The increased self-government of the members is a modern trend, but it can on occasion be aimed at the suppression of yet smaller parts.

In recent times we have seen the formation of fixed or increasingly close federal relationships; and we have seen the loosening of federations to a fixed point of stabilisation or towards complete disintegration. It is only possible to evaluate such a development after examining the state of freedom as well as the tendencies of the national and supra-national structures. For example, it can be said that the transformation of the British Empire into a British Commonwealth of Nations, although a loosening of the links, has been a positive step; but its complete disintegration could produce negative results as well. In the United States the federal structure has many elements of freedom, but there are cases when a particular state claims prerogatives that can be retrograde or conserve oppression. At the same time the increasing power of the federal authority coincides with an increasingly united American nation.

So it is of doubtful benefit to try to create or maintain federations when there is a lack of willing, or when there are mutual national differences. Federation is not a miracle drug or a happy ending to a novel. It does not abolish problems, but adds a multitude of new ones. It is unwise to take it on half-heartedly with a load of unsettled problems, or to maintain it at any cost simply for its own sake. There is no proof that large units make a better starting point for greater integration than small ones, and there are indications to show that nations need to be clearly formed if they are to be able to merge into a viable supra-national form. And nations may have to reject federations which are unable to offer the perspective of nation-formation and social progress together.

We have seen how the colonial empires fell apart, federation-like formations mushroomed, and their adversities showed up more failures than successes. All this proves that a successful federation must have freedom, self-government and voluntary participation, it must have a clear common goal and the compliance of the federal organisation with the real tendencies of nation-formation or supra-national integration, and it must have the clear demarcation of the separate national frameworks.

Criticism of self-determination and the nation state by comparison with the former empires

Critics of the principle of self-determination and the nation state tend to recall the virtues of units such as the Hapsburg Empire, which have been destroyed by self-determination, and the disharmonies that existed when colonial empires were replaced by new independent states. The Hapsburg Empire and similar units are then nostalgically recalled, by both privileged and ordinary people, for their greater security, broader perspectives and higher cultural level. It must not be forgotten that such empires were built on the monarchic-aristocratic principle, or on racial superiority; but the fact remains that they were accepted by the majority, and they could rely on a more solid authority and function more easily and cheaply than those recent states which are sometimes backward, still burdened with tribal situations, and still trying to build a national state, a national intelligence and a national administration on inadequate foundations.

But this does not take us far; there is no longer a choice between the old, discredited principles and the trend towards the nation state with common conviction leading to the justification of the demarcation between power spheres. Experience has shown that once mass movement makes the demand for the justification of power, the structures of dominance and the principles supporting them are questioned by both those in power and the sufferers of power, and no smooth administration can help them. Once mass movement demands a nation state there is no consolidation that will help those larger forms of integration that are not sustained by communal consciousness and mass emotion. Although there was a measure of integration in the multi-national structures of the extinct empires, the principles of monarchic-feudal legitimacy or of racial superiority restricted this measure; but the empires that were dissolved more or less peacefully allowed self-determination to be substituted for their outdated principles and thus made way for the necessary integration.

Good fortune may keep a shaky structure standing for a long time, and it would have been conceivable for many of these empires to exist still. But ultimately they would have had to fall before the first real storm or, sooner or later, to allow themselves to be pulled down. Those who wish nostalgically that these empires were still with us are yearning for the order and security, not for the oppression, arrogance, exploitation and dismissal of national demands which prepared the downfall of these structures.

Of course the downfall of the old integration, though a prerequisite, holds no guarantee of the birth of a new and healthier one. If for some reason there is no outward stability and clear demarcation, no inner progress towards freedom in the newly evolved smaller units, and no integration between these untis that is both voluntary and meets real requirements, then 'Balkanisation' follows – the very process that seems to justify the former large units. And yet it is wrong to say that the liquidation of colonial empires ought not to have been so hasty. Instead this liquidation ought to have been effected rather more thoughtfully, with more uniformity and based more on principles. But such a statement is meaningless except as a warning for the future.

The inevitability of the principles of sovereignty of the people and self-determination as a step on the road to international integration

Again and again we meet the pull of sovereignty of the people and self-determination, the twin principles of a social organisation based on freedom and equal human dignity, and this no matter how much other important considerations try to draw us away. It appears that there is no other principle that is rooted in common conviction and that could ensure the social and psychological conditions of legitimacy, and the necessary inner and outer organisation. And there appears to be nothing that could or should replace these in the foreseeable future.

We must emphasise that there is today a strong common conviction which in critical foreign and domestic politics accepts the verdict of the people, so long as this is expressed in a suitable form, as a sacrosanct verdict; but it does not similarly accept the sentences pronounced by kings, noblemen and technocrats. All criticisms marshalled against self-determination are reminiscent of the recurring theories and moods of disillusion of the past 300 years that have frequently declared the twilight of self-determination as the basic principle of the inner organisations of the state. But always it was found that these critics intended to replace the sovereignty of the people with something inferior; and sovereignty of the people would arise with renewed strength, and similarly with the counterpart of sovereignty of the people – self-determination.

The undistorted application of the principles derived from the concept of democratic freedom may well lessen the threat of war, even amongst a multitude of states, and even more than the application of the greatest possible power. So we have reason to believe that a more effective, if less spectacular, way to bring about peaceful coexistence, is to promote a society based on self-determination with a stable balance between the multitude of states. This is not meant to diminish any constructive ideas on a world state, world élite, or higher forms of integration. But no matter how swift the appearance of a central global power may be, before it comes the threat of a nuclear holocaust must be averted by the present international community formed by nation states. So the task we have before us is to settle the problems with self-determination as the basic principle of today's international community, without waiting for a prospective international integration.

[7]

Other Principles of State-Formation and Territorial Settlement in Supposed Rivalry with Self-Determination

The national principle and its variants: theories of national, historic, ethnic and other identities

There are other, much less ambitious, challenges to the principle of self-determination as it is in actual political practice. Sometimes the concepts which formulate the principle are interpreted in such a way as to produce contradictions within it, which may be done in good faith, in pursuit of an unbiased solution, or it may be done for purposes of political power, when questions of state-formation or territorial settlements are involved.

The most important of the challenges comes from the national principle and its variants – the principle of nationalities or the populist concept (Volkstum). These have been referred to throughout the nineteenth and twentieth centuries in a variety of contexts, but always in connection with state-formation and territorial disputes and mainly with regard to the principle of self-determination, which confirms that, in the present stage of social evolution, self-determination usually equates with the communal will to form a nation state. The national principle and its variants are simply references to those objective criteria which any nation-formation based on self-determination follows.

The expression 'national principle' places emphasis on an historically evolved political framework; while 'populism' relies on ethnic and linguistic criteria – concepts that were not sufficiently considered by the principle of nationalities in the nineteenth century. The difference between the two criteria has recently appeared as a confrontation between historic and ethnic principles. In the West and North of Europe, and many other parts of the world, nation-formation has generally followed the political boundaries established by history – boundaries that may have been drawn by dynastic and military incident, but stable before the appearance of the mass movements of democratism. On the other hand, in Central and Eastern Europe, and some other places, nation-formation ignored the historic boundaries which had become unstable, and began to adopt ethnic and linguistic boundaries. This readily happens when democratic and national mass movements are faced by unstable, disputed state borders. In exceptional cases religion may be a factor in nation-formation, but usually coinciding with linguistic or other factors.

Wherever the progress of nation-formation is problem-free these criteria may serve as a basis for settlement, without the question being put formally to the people; though such solutions could not be considered as an alternative to the basic democratic principle of self-determination. Wherever these criteria have seemed to clash with self-determination there have been problems concerned with the transitional period of nation-formation, or some crisis in progress, or a border dispute; or there was the intervention of opposing forces, the appearance of nationalistic ideologies and, through all these the process of nation-formation being either misunderstood or misrepresented.

The three examples which follow may be useful.

(i) The first example is an illustration of the principle of self-determination in conflict with the historic principle, a variant of the national principle, which happened whenever the ethnic principle competed with the historic as a basis for nation-formation. This happened in Central and Eastern Europe where, after some vacillation, nation-formation progressed along linguistic divides after having diverged from the rather shaky historic frameworks of the Holy Roman Empire, the historic Kingdom of Poland, and Hungary. Attempts were made to protect the historic state boundaries with nationalistic ideology, which involved a rather futile confrontation with the ethnic principle supported by self-determination. In practice this meant that the historic state structure was imposed, anti-democratically, on people who spoke different languages.

(ii) The principle of self-determination came into conflict with the ethnic principles, as a variant of the national one, wherever the process of nation-formation was led by developments of history away from the ethnic borders. A classic example of this is the case of Alsace-Lorraine. Through historic processes, this country was torn from the Germans without regard to its ethnic and historic ties with them, to become part of France. In 1814, when the people of the Rhineland received the Prussians and Austrians as deliverers, Alsace and Lorraine remained as hostile to them as they were to France. The German intelligentsia failed to understand why the German-speaking people of Alsace and Lorraine would not take part in the formation of the German nation, which evolved mainly on linguistic lines, and Goerres and generations of Germans after him considered this a temporary aberration or cultural snobbishness that would have to be cured. In this instance nationalistic ideology, using the ethnic principle (Volkstum) as absolute, opposed a new political link, historically evolved and supported by self-determination and the process of nation-formation. The exponents of this concept were trying to impose anti-democratically an alien political consciousness upon part of the people in Alsace and Lorraine. This shows how, in extreme cases where the historic or ethnic principles have no connection with self-determination or with the process and vacillations of nation-formation, any reference to these principles is usually motivated by power claims or a desire to dominate, and is irrelevant from the national point of view or from that of self-determination. The historic principle does not confer the right to re-establish long-defunct situations; but it formulates the political links that have evolved through history and are still effective. The ethnic principle can only be used to form states on the basis of ethnic or linguistic situations when those situations coincide with social and political progress and, again, not as an arbitrary right. It is clear that in both these cases the principle of self-determination and the national criteria it supports are superior to the opposing criteria of the historic and ethnic principles.

(iii) The third example is more complex: politically primitive communities where the principle of self-determination appears to clash with other principles. Here there is no claim to self-determination on the part of the majority of the population; this claim is voiced only by social and political leaders and the intelligentsia. Yet it is almost always possible to see the criteria and directions that will be decisive: generally some existing power interest that appeals to the will of the people – almost always in bad faith – maintaining that the decent ordinary man is not interested in state, border, independence or the fight for freedom, but only in work, peace and prosperity. Using propaganda, and even plebiscites with deliberately misleading questions, self-determination can be used to disrupt the process of nation-formation. Here it is necessary that the visible historic, ethnic or other criteria of nation-formation be given priority over 'self-determination' used in bad faith.

Thus, in disputes over state-formation or territories, and especially the new borders of the former colonial countries, it is not convincing to argue that the national frontiers have been drawn arbitrarily and with caprice. Where these frontiers have beome stable and been followed with the movement towards democracy and nation-formation, this may not be harmful, but it may cause trouble where these processes meet with unstable boundaries, and where arbitrary frontiers conflict with growing or established national consciousness. This will be seen with each of the new countries of the former colonial territories, whether the boundaries are inherited from the colonies (which usually has no major historical significance), or whether there are opposing influences of nation-formation against which the state structures might react with physical force and with national ideologies aimed at domination.

Practical considerations in state-formation and territorial problems

From the viewpoint of self-determination, one must be cautious when seemingly practical and realistic considerations are used for state-formation and territorial settlement, as they can be disguises of an aspiration to power, domination or conquest. Such considerations may be economic, geographical, concerned with communications, or strategic, the last of which so obviously serves one-sided interests that it has been refuted by all statesmen and experts of integrity. In most cases the other three considerations are also disguises made to seem practical, but they are often applied usefully by well-meaning experts in forming a new state or settling a territorial dispute, and sometimes in the best interests of the people.

But it can be misleading to allow these practical considerations to be entangled with the principles of self-determination and nation-formation. It makes it appear as if there were a choice between a multitude of considerations, with self-determination as but one of many, allowing all practical propositions to be freely weighed against each other; while the actual paramount importance is to apply only those principles which were endowed with legitimacy by common conviction, for only these can secure loyalty to the new state structure or frontiers. Purely practical considerations must not be allowed to override questions tht mobilise public opinion and rouse strong communal feeling — it would be like ordering a Baptist family to convert to Anglicanism because the church is nearer their house than the chapel. The Soviet Union has drawn her inner political borders on ethnic grounds rather than on economic and practical ones — although economic factors are regarded as important — and in so doing she has rightly applied the nationality principle. The economic failings of a state structure or national frontiers should be remedied by economic integration, not by tampering with the structures; and this meets with the least opposition if the state's framework follows the national one.

The Mosul dispute is a classic example of the confusing effect of expertise on considerations of self-determination, nationality and practicality. In their report to the League of Nations, the experts claimed that a survey showed the will of the people to be in favour of the stronger government. The population of the territory in question wanted to belong to Iraq if Great Britain stayed there, as they considered Great Britain the stronger power; but they preferred Turkey if the British withdrew from Iraq, Turkey then having the stronger government. The territory was eventually granted to Iraq, which was then a British Mandate. At first sight the argument seems logical; but it becomes grotesque when we ask if the whole question should not have been revived when Britain eventually withdrew from Iraq. And the nonsense in the argument is deeper than this. When the so-called will of the people considers strength alone to be the decisive factor in a question of allegiance, the country is in a pre-self-determination stage and its will is therefore irrelevant so far as self-determination is concerned. In such a case neither this kind of will nor any other point of practicality should be consulted; only the discernible trends of nation-formation must be used as yardsticks for decisions.

All in all, we must conclude that principles of state-formation or territorial settlement which claim to be alternatives to self-determination can be shown to be either derived from self-determination or else they represent concepts arising from misrepresentation.

[8]

Self-Determination as Opposed to the Territorial Integrity of States

Refutation of the subversive effect of the principle of self-determination by the existing state powers

An argument used against the principle of self-determination that is not based on another principle but is raised from the viewpoint of 'realpolitik', condemns self-determination for being subversive, interfering with internal affairs and threatening war. Hitler used this kind of claim. It covers all kinds of movement aimed at independence, self-determination or separation. The argument is reinforced by the claim that self-determination is not built into international law, and even in the United Nations Charter it is confined to a general declaration of principle – so no legal claims can be based on it.

There is also an argument that reserves self-determination for the use of entire nations which demand their independence, or for communities with a relatively high level of state organisation, while denying it to the people, to amorphous groups or fragments of communities without a political framework.

While we disentangle these arguments, we must emphasise the importance of territorial stability to the international community. It is in the desire for this that states bear the responsibilities of international law, and it is why they are so sensitive over their own territorial *status quo,* their territorial integrity. Because of this sensitivity, they are inclined to identify their physical existence with their territory: to see signs of strength if it is increased, and weakness or annihilation if there is a loss. In this there is an almost symbolic significance attached to the cartographic appearance of the actual or desired territory; and, through mass education and map-making, this affects a wide circle of people.

In this outlook there is a desire to own and dominate that is a pre-self-determination, anti-democratic trait. It is more democratic to regard the country first and foremost as the sum of all citizens claiming allegiance to it, or, perhaps, as the sum of their homes. But this territory-centred outlook is subscribed to by the masses as much as the representatives of power, and particularly in nations that have experienced threats to their existence.

For social and political communities to be prepared to consider claims to self-determination against their own states, they must have absorbed democratism totally and have become politically mature and sensitive to concepts transcending physical existence. It shows a relatively high regard for the principle of self-determination when a state appears inclined to give up geographically and culturally remote colonies that were never integral parts of the mother country, or when it is willing to recognise the right to separation of its autonomous parts. When a greater measure of self-determination is claimed by territories that are geographically linked to the mother country, there is generally more resistance, even though they may be constitutionally separate, self-governing units. And claims to self-determination by a group of people with their own national allegiance but living in part of the mother country are hardly ever recognised by even the most democratic societies, except by way of moral and legal condemnation.

So territorial self-government is a highly explosive issue. States are reluctant to allow territorial self-government, for it transforms an amorphous group of people whose claims were hitherto domestic matters into a visibly separate national identity, into a nation or the seeds of a nation; and this group of people would then be more able to invoke the principle of self-determination, to extend its claims and even take them to an international forum. And territorial self-government actually puts such a group of people on the map and, with separatist trends, can provide the draft of new frontiers.

This seems to suggest that claims made on the basis of the principle of self-determination are, to an extent, contrary to one of the most important fundamental principles of international law: the territorial integrity of states. It would appear that self-determination and territorial stability were incompatible principles.

The necessity of self-determination for existing states as a justifying and stabilising force

In the last analysis, rejection of the right to self-determination by existing states is divorced from any consideration of principle, dogma or legality. Such rejection reflects the desire of organisations to maintain their physical powers, and their opposition to all doctrinaire views, to all views based on principles. At risk of an international legal explosion, this is occasionally carried to extremes with insistence on the unconditional sanctity of a *status quo* as if there were some sort of 'divine right' of governments to the loyalty of all citizens – but this has no support from the common conviction. This age-old argument is used by states that have stability, order, legality and progress; but it is also used by tyrannies, colonial or racial supremacies, and occupying forces to defend their possessions and their volatile situations. And the shakier the moral, conceptual and legal foundations of the powers using this argument, the more vociferous is their insistence on their legal and 'divine' right to the loyalty of their citizens, and their condemnation of disloyalty and the external factors that incite it.

We may say that power organisations so lacking in legality should not expect the protection of international law simply on the basis of territorial integrity. But it is not so simple as that. International law has an external criterion for deciding the states entitled to protection: that the power must be stable and organised. And this criterion is one that can be achieved through tyranny or conquest. This sort of justification is not enough for states today. Whether or not it is really so, they all claim that the entire population with unanimous self-determining will wishes to maintain the *status quo*, which embodies their national ambitions. Parallel to this is a growing international view that would limit the protection of international view that would limit the protection of internation law to states which not only satisfy the criteria of stability and formal legality, but are also able to secure a minimum of human rights, democracy and self-determination.

The idea of an international organisation of states based on democratic institutions emerged after the First World War. It becomes increasingly difficult to make this effective as more politically and culturally diverse countries are included, countries with different interpretations of the meaning of democracy. In this situation states and groups of states are inclined to expect higher standards of human rights, democracy and self-determination from their opponents, and to be a great deal less exacting when it comes to their friends. However, after the lessons of fascism and the Second World War, an international forum more frequently exists between ideologically differing states and political regimes, which join in condemning rule without a minimum requirement of democracy. It is through this that the territorial integrity of long-established colonial empires has been discounted.

So a vicious circle of contradictions has appeared. Existing states may appeal to international law against claims on their territories made in the name of self-determination; but rather than invalidating the principle of self-determination, their appeal will only be met if they are exponents of human rights, democracy and self-determination. At the same time, the more a state is stable, democratic and rooted in self-determination, the more it is inclined to consider claims of self-determination against itself; while the shakier the power, the louder is the condemnation of such opposition to its superiority.

It seems, then, that self-determination has both a subversive and a justifying role. Those who overestimate the disruptive elements – which may be done in an anxiety for peace – also overestimate the stability of *de facto* situations that are not founded in the principle; and they underestimate the real stabilising force of self-determination and the disruptive effects of violation of the principle.

Self-determination is a stabilising force in that the strength it gives to situations is greater than the existing power relationships, and also it can quickly stabilise and make permanent the changes that are provoked by or favourable to it. The tolerable stability of the legal orders and territories in our world is due to the fact that they are essentially complying with the principle of self-determination. The majority of people live in countries they want to live in, and accept authority as a matter of course. If for any reason there were less concord between the *status quo* and self-determination, and if for lack of self-determination the state and national frontiers were supported only by power and international law, we cannot estimate the extent of the shocks and conflicts that could follow. And although it may not be obvious, in most of the world the aggressiveness of governments is contained through the principle of self-determination being the only politically acceptable title to expansion. If this were not so, governments with their 'divine rights' would produce a far more chaotic international systems and would disrupt the *status quo* far more than is possible with the backing of the principle of self-determination.

On the other hand, violation of self-determination provokes effects that reach beyond the population concerned, extending to rival countries and their populations. This is shown when national consciousness, derived from self-determination, turns against democracy, and it is particularly dangerous in countries that are in the process of being democratised and whose existence is threatened. Minorities who are disloyal, or allegedly so, provide an excuse for the suspension of freedoms which harms the democracy of the whole country. Claims to self-determination which have not been peacefully satisfied may cause policies that are dangerous and anti-democratic, externally and internally. Finally, a hopeless claim to self-determination will lead peoples to embark on disillusioned movements and ideologies which turn against freedom.

The twin functions of self-determination: the present supremacy of the justifying and stabilising function, and the inevitability of the subversive and revolutionising function

So, like all governing principles, self-determination does not attack stability any more than change does. But it contains a duality: it has a justifying, stabilising, conserving effect and it has a criticising, subversive, revolutionising one. It is only the emphasis that occasionally shifts. All governing principles are at first rather revolutionising; but once generally adopted they become more stabilising. Both aspects are important. Even in the most revolutionary moments the governing principle can be fruitful only if it has the prospect of stability before it; but after consolidation it is essential that it remains open to change. Change at the temporary expense of stability can serve a more lasting stability in the long run. There is no point at which a principle, launched as a revolutionary force, can deny criticism or freeze into a concept justifying the *status quo*.

The principle of self-determination has already passed the revolutionary stage – the stage when it overcame the principles of monarchic-feudal legitimacy in Europe and racial superiority in the world at large, redrawing the maps of America in the eighteenth and nineteenth centuries, of Europe after the First World War, and of Africa and part of Asia after the Second. On the whole, self-determination is now more stabilising than subversive. Wherever it is invoked to bring about change it is in an endeavour to improve and extend an accepted situation, or to correct certain disharmonies, and it is not a matter of a new governing principle bringing downfall to an established order. But the question of the correct application of the principle will certainly recur, mainly in connection with newly independent or still-dependent colonies and peoples. Here the subversive, revolutionising aspects temporarily arise: questions of oppressed nations, peoples or colonies groping for independence; questions of a just national border; the impossibility of loyalty to the existing state.

Like all governing principles, self-determination has to pay for its stabilising effects. While it is more effective than the pure *status quo* and power position, and while it confirms and justifies situations within its ambit, by dint of being a principle it condemns, subverts, revolutionises those who are non-compliant. Today there are not very many of these cases, and when they occur the principle of self-determination prescribes changes which serve to eliminate or to reform such situations.

For all the primary stabilising effect of self-determination, no amount of dislike, resentment or condemnation will remove these revolutionising, subversive side effects. If they are ignored and not given the opportunity of manifesting themselves through well-organised channels, they will appear in disorganised, unregulated ways. Whatever we do there will be such problems; but this is similar to the way in which, under a constitution that declares equal rights for all citizens, there should continue to be civil rights movements organised by people who feel underprivileged.

There is another sense in which self-determination cannot be restricted. It cannot be confined to nations alone, excluding people without such a political structure. We cannot say that self-determination is right only for those who already have it and the rest might as well forget it. Every nation was first a people who decided to become a nation, or to join one, no matter whether the process were a sudden one or a slow political progression.

Though self-determination shows the desire for political organisation, the two are not interdependent. Just as there are peoples who have no political organisation and yet have developed a strong claim to self-determination or separate nationhood, there are also communities who have a political organisation and territorial autonomy but who are devoid of any claim to self-determination or separate nationhood, much less separation. Such is the case with the member states of the United States and of Brazil.

A community with its own political organisation, administration and representative bodies will obviously find it easier to achieve self-determination than one without these. But if we try to limit the right to self-determination purely to those communities that have such political institutions, we open the door to dangerous political misconceptions. In this case every state would be justified in believing – as some actually do – that grants of territorial self-government to a minority or to part of its own territory would pave the way to self-determination and even separation. Also, if a state rejected a claim to self-government, or withdrew it once given, it would be defending its territorial integrity and denying reality to claims of self-determination against itself.

But territorial self-government is not the cause of a separatist movement. At most it shows whether the movement aims simply at self-government or at national separation. If self-government is denied to such a community the problem only grows more acute; and there are many instances in which the denial of territorial self-government has given impetus to national separatist movements.

So the occasional appearance of movements aimed at the formation of new states or at effecting territorial changes is inevitable under the rule of the principle of self-determination. The question only is how to settle conflicts that arise out of such movements.

The solution of conflicts between self-determination and territorial stability

There is no question of confrontation between the principles of self-determination and of territorial stability, and here lies the solution to the apparent contradictions. The principle of territorial stability cannot invalidate that of self-determination, as self-determination is the ultimate governing principle, whereas territorial stability is not so much a principle as the institutional reality of international law. We could say that compliance with the principle of self-determination is the essence, the real legitimacy of a *status quo,* while territoral stability stands for formal, institutionalised legitimacy.

In the establishment of the principle of self-determination there was no battle with territorial stability; the battle was with monarchic-feudal legitimacy, which was based on different concepts – and this is now over with the triumph of self-determination. But the actual struggle for territorial stability is a perennial contest between each principle and the institution built upon it: there is no once-and-for-all victory or defeat. It is a contest between the essence and the form of legitimacy. The institution cannot invalidate the principle, as its function is to stabilise the situations created by the principle. On the other hand, the principle can only be effective through the institution, and for this it has both to overcome and to tolerate the crudity and rigidity of the institution. In actual situations this results in a multitude of problems, clashes, breaches of the principle and compromises. However, the principle cannot allow its stipulations to be blunted or distorted through its institutions; nor can the institution allow the situation to become unstable because of adjustments needed to give full effect to the principle. This is why there can be no clear distinction between domestic affairs in which outside interference is forbidden by the territorial integrity of states, and the right to self-determination by the peoples.

There is no abstract formula independent of time and place to solve such seeming contradictions; but there are generally valid solutions to the problems of making a given principle effective.

To formulate such answers concerning the principle of self-determination and of international territorial stability, we must return to the idea that, in a sense, the international community, the ensemble of states and their territorial status together play the role of the constitution. Every constitution is, in principle, unchangeable, and alterations are exceptional, and here is the problem of the subversive effect of self-determination. Can the constitution be criticised, and is it right to suggest changes? Undoubtedly it is wrong to do this so often as to let it be forgotten that the constitution is, generally speaking, not meant to be changed; but it is necessary whenever there is a danger that a stipulation or institution of the constitution may become false or ineffectual, with risk of shaking the whole edifice.

A few propositions may serve as guidelines in the event of clashes between the principle of self-determination as the source of essential legitimacy in the international community, and the institution of territorial stability, i.e. the formal legitimacy of the the international community:

(i) The main function of the principle of self-determination is to help peoples to become well-defined nations, recognised by the international community, wherever this has not as yet happened, speedily and simply. The principle gives a clear and conceptual foundation for the formation of the basic units of the international community, the individual states. Also it serves to fix points of orientation for the loyalty of the individual. So it is desirable that all changes are brought about by the practical application of self-determination, in essence and circumstances, and that they should be peaceful, even from the viewpoint of territorial stability.

(ii) Given the structure and character of the international community, every state-formation, every territorial change is an exceptional event.

The fact that it is desirable for there to be changes in compliance with self-determination does not mean that the peoples should constantly re-determine their future. Just as sovereignty of the people works through decisive expressions of will at critical moments, and does not mean the constant participation of the people in the actual exercise of power, similarly the principle of self-determination cannot mean plebiscites for every recurring change so far as states and their borders are concerned; it is, rather, a governing principle to be applied in settling disputes. When people make a principle, an ideology of the need for the growth of state structures, or the external fluidity of borders — as with fascist regimes — this is in contradiction with the spirit of international law.

(iii) If we are to avert conflicts developing from the occasional clashes between the legal institution of territorial integrity and the requirements of self-determination, we must find procedures – the more peaceful the better — which by incorporating certain changes and increasing stability can meet the requirements of self-determination.

(iv) Given the present structure of the international community, these cannot be ordinary procedures through which some agency may impose binding decisions over state-formations and territorial changes on the basis of self-determination, enforcing them on all parties concerned. As these changes are to be exceptional, the procedures must also be exceptional.

(v) Such exceptional — although not rare — cases are those in which the problems are so extensive as to transcend the power of individual states; or when disputes are so complex or dangerous as to make it necessary for changes to be effected on the basis of self-determination, given that the circumstances make this possible.

This is where the question of how to apply the principle arises.

Problems of the application of the principle of self-determination, and the lack of institutions and procedures for putting it into practice

Now for the most common objection against the principle of self-determination: the assertion that the problems of applying it are all but insoluble — it is difficult to establish what exactly is the will of the community, and anyhow it is liable to change; questions can be formulated and put before the population in bad faith; the criteria of state-formation and demarcation are not easy to establish; groups with opposing wills are geographically mixed, or may have changed their locations, giving rise to the danger that no just borders can be drawn and that yet further claims to new state-formation may be made; and so forth.

All these problems are concerned with putting the principle into practice, and undoubtedly, like other principles, there are problems in applying self-determination; but they are rather less than the problems of applying other, similar principles. For example, there are between one and two hundred sections in constitutional law which are devoted to the constitutional principle of sovereignty of the people; and again there are hundreds of clauses of civil law and legal procedure concerned with the principle of private property.

The problems arising from the application of the principle of self-determination are largely these: When does the principle entitle a group of people to create their independent state, and when does the population of a certain territory have the right to join the state of their choice? How should the will of the people manifest itself, what facts and characteristic features make this clear, and when is it necessary to ask the population formally? If the common will can be taken for granted, what criteria can be used to measure it in individual cases? On the occasion of a plebiscite, how are questions to be formulated fairly and realistically? Is it permissible, and if so when, to repeat the questions? How are the answers of the voters to be interpreted if they raise problems of their own? What is the solution for territories with mixed populations or clashing wills? What territories must be considered indivisible and decided on a majority basis, and what territories can or must be divided after a plebiscite? What is to be done if the population has voluntarily or otherwise changed its domicile and resettled elsewhere, and what kind of self-determination can a group of people claim over a territory where it has only recently arrived but has already settled down in? How are all these facts and criteria to be clarified and how should decisions be carried out?

In order to answer all these questions, some thrity or forty rules need to be formulated. Commissions and experts have so far failed to do this, and they have failed to be thorough enough when questions of state-formation or territorial changes have had to be considered. But the chief obstacle is not so much the lack of rules as the absence of competent bodies and procedures.

Rules provide no precondition for the application of the principle of self-determination, but rather they result from the process of putting the principle into practice, and they are gradually worked out in the the course of finding practical solutions to actual problems, through an established process, by a competent agency. In the early development of law, procedure precedes codified law. Barna Horvath put it well when he said that the procedure manages to steer between the extremes of applying the generally accepted principles too rigidly or too loosely, and it guides rules through the pitfalls of over-stabilising or over-revolutionising, rules that are made necessary by the friction between the principle and reality.

The difficulty of applying self-determination is not that the problems are unsurmountable – their solutions have never yet been attempted; and it is not because absolute justice cannot be attained in concrete questions –

for this is clearly impossible in any dispute or law suit – and justice is still being done. The difficulty is rather that there is no procedure, no agencies in the internatonal community that are primarily designed to solve these problems. The simple procedures that do exist for state-formation or territorial adjustments are the legacy of an earlier outlook and system. In the few cases where improvised bodies have taken a stand over questions related to self-determination, they have not so far provided the rudiments for procedural methods, agencies and rules to evolve on a permanent basis.

So we are back with that vital problem of all constitutions: the procedures through which situations that are meant to be permanent can, in exceptions, be altered. A legal system with no procedures for bringing about exceptional changes is highly unsatisfactory, even though it recognises self-determination as governing the permanent institutions such as the community of nations and their territorial status.

Some jurists see no place for the principle of self-determination in the system of international law, and we can now see that this is because it has no institutional, procedural support. If we ask whether sovereignty of the people – the counterpart of self-determination – has any legal significance, a place in the legal systems of individual states, we may observe that there are some constitutions that do not so much as mention it, yet every modern constitution has a multitude of legal institutions and procedures that can only be understood as a function of the principle of sovereignty of the people. Thus, even if the principle is not part of law, it is the point of reference, the ultimate reason and foundation for a number of laws. But it is useless insisting that the principle of self-determination is the only possible foundation of the most important elements of the international constitution, the ensemble of states and their territorial status, if there are insufficient institutional and procedural forms for putting it into effect.

Now we can find a common denominator to all the difficulties and objections concerning the principle of self-determination. The causes are not in the principle itself, but in its failure to be put into effect. The difficulties are characteristic manifestations of conceptual and practical human activity that has not been clearly thought out. And since the principle of self-determination is the only possible principle of state-formation and territorial adjustment, the shortcomings of the way it is applied – the lack of institutions and procedures through which it could be properly applied – lead to grave crises, disillusionment, political hysteria and international conflicts. And because the ever-recurring theme of these conflicts is the principle of self-determination, we doubt the principle itself, the principle we cannot do without.

We still have the long-overdue task of forming the institutes and procedures that are able to further the progress and application of the principle of self-determination, and that can give it the ability to stabilise situations and to bring about exceptional changes. For this we must first consider the agencies, procedures and rules that are at present available for the international community to settle questions of state-formation, and territorial adjustments and other political issues.

[9]

The Inadequacy of Present-day Methods for Settling Political Disputes

Procedures for state-formation and territorial settlement in the past and present

In summing up the existing procedures of international law, we found that the system of rules and legal structure of recent European monarchies still contains some validity. And the basic principle behind these, and behind the aristocratic republics, was monarchic-feudal legitimacy. The problems of applying this principle were seen mainly in the interpretation of laws of succession, dynastic agreements, decisions over territories without a sovereign, the discovery of the essence of feudal rights and relationships. Monarchic-feudal Europe conceived a rather primitive yet, by the time of the Congress of Vienna, a logically constructed system for settling these problems. This consisted of rules and laws, and explicit or implicit conventions.

For territorial adjustments between states, agreement was required between sovereigns confident in the loyalty of their subjects; any shifts in the balance could be corrected through mediation by a third power or though territorial exchange. For the formation of new states, existing ones would have to recognise them and enter into diplomatic relations with them. Disputes not settled by peaceful solutions were settled by a duel-like procedural war, restricted to professional armies, which would lead to a peace treaty through negotiation. The treaty would be confined to the settlement of the dispute and would not be exploited to the extreme by the victor. Questions of sovereignty over unclaimed territories, worsening crises between weaker states, complex state-formations or territorial adjustments, or other questions concerning the entire community were settled by the assembly of powers.

This system was closer to the code of honour or duelling of an aristocratic club than to a modern legal system, but it worked in applying the principle of monarchic-feudal legitimacy – on the whole faithfully, and flexibly according to the balance of power. The solutions were durable and accepted by both sovereigns and their subjects, and the system more or less survived until the sovereigns dealt it a mortal blow by launching world war with compulsory military service.

The rules and procedures were not entirely invalidated by the collapse of the European monarchic system in 1918, as by then the international law of the monarchies had become universal international law, accepted by most European and overseas constitutional monarchies and representative republics. However, the rise of the principle of self-determination made it in some respects contradictory and unable to function, without providing a new system that could function beside, or in place of, the old one. But after the two World Wars, the League of Nations, and then the United Nations and a number of international specialist agencies and the permanent International Court of Justice developed from the more broadly based institutions of the new global community of states. Even so, the procedure and organisation governing new state-formations and territorial settlements is a combination of the often unworkable old systems and the still inadequate new procedures.

This combination is less satisfactory than the old system when it existed alone:

(i) War became total, and incapable of settling disputes. Its complete abolition is the central purpose of international law and policies – and yet it is still with us, institutionalised and fundamentally unchanged.

(ii) Insurrection has become a more frequent means of achieving self-determination and, without other procedures to replace it, cannot be completely ruled out – although one would not wish it to become institutionalised and recurrent.

(iii) International police forces have been used seldom and with little success, for the purpose of averting wars – mostly because of lack of concord amongst the great powers.

(iv) The mechanics and spirit of international negotiation for international agreement have seriously deteriorated; and, for legitimising state-formations and territorial adjustments, the authority of international agreement has waned without anything to replace it.

(v) Recognition and diplomatic relations, once helpful in stabilising newly formed states, have deteriorated into capriciously used political weapons.

(vi) International guarantee of minority rights and territorial self-government – a useful second-best to self-determination – has not always been able to count on the loyalty of a population demanding self-determination.

(vii) Population exchanges – that have resulted from this failure – if widely applied and without suitable guarantee, would destroy territorial legitimacy, or the right of peoples to be masters of their land.

(viii) Plebiscites have proved to be a useful but sensitive and easily distorted institution, and so far they have been applied arbitrarily and sometimes without those impartial forums that are essential for the proper functioning of a referendum.

(ix) The concert of powers, the supreme governing agency until the First World War, has been increasingly unable to meet the requirements of great power agreement and top-level decision. When it does function, it is only to be used by the great powers to circumvent, for some reason of their own, the existing and more institutionalised procedures of global institutions.

(x) The Security Council, which was to embody the modern version of the great power agreement, is often less energetic and effectual, despite its institutional stability, than its predecessor, the concert of powers. It barely discharges its duties in averting war; its police function has not properly begun; and its general governing function is confined to temporary stop-gap solutions, far inferior to the functioning of the one-time concert of great powers.

(xi) Mediation, significant for its role in establishing agreement among the great powers, has been greatly strengthened by the powers of the Secretary General of the United Nations.

(xii) The International Court of Justice and lesser international courts were conceived as impartial forums, but they do not go beyond the strict application of codified international law to act as political arbitrators.

(xiii) It has so far been impossible to fill the void thus created with the institution of impartial international political arbitration.

Let us now examine these points individually.

War which became an absurdity and has yet stayed with us

By the eighteenth century war had developed a highly civilised code, that had standing for the civil population and professional soldier alike; but from the nineteenth century this degenerated increasingly towards total warfare. The first stage in this degeneracy was the introduction of compulsory military service, which involved the whole population in war. This development was considered to run parallel to the political democratisation of the masses.

The next logical step was the universal people's war, meaning a fight, using every conceivable means, against foreign invading armies; and this happened with increasing frequency. An invading army was no longer seen as representing a duel between a neighbouring king and one's own; now it was seen as the lawless aggression of a whole neighbouring people. Reaction to this came as armies on enemy soil classified all civilians, partisans or resistants who opposed them as 'snipers'; and this multiplied the atrocities and extended war to even wider groups of people.

At the same time, the basic contradiction between such 'democratisation' of war and the democratisation of freedom has become more obvious. It had been possible for martial gentlemen and professional soldiers to consider the killing and mutual danger as a part of duelling, a kind of sport. But now, for the masses, war was seen as something that must be avoided, or once started must be carried through to the total annihilation of the enemy. Compulsory military service and the universal people's war were followed by submarine war, starvation of civilian populations, aerial bombing of the hinterland — developments that could only facetiously be called further democratisation of warfare.

By the end of the First World War it was recognised that war was the greatest enemy of human progress and happiness, and its prevention became the chief purpose of all global organisations since then. The development of nuclear warfare emphasised the importance of prevention, and with it the 'progress' of war has theoretically reached its peak. And now there is limited time to work out the alternatives before us. Fear has brought a measure of sobriety and a halt at the point called the 'balance of terror'. But this can only continue so long as technical progress in nuclear warfare implies that the victor must accept similar destruction to the vanquished, and so victory is an illusion.

But politicians and people are defenceless against technical developments that could upset this balance of terror and even make pre-emptive war attractive. We are defenceless but not innocent in the face of this possibility: a proportion of politicians and public opinion have considered the political and military superiority of their own side as desirable and have pressed science and technology for such developments, often with the sincere belief that the weapons would only threaten peace if they were in the hands of the opposing party. So it is vital that a measure of international organisation should be used to lessen the threat of nuclear war.

The motive behind the post-Second World War charters of world organisations was the attempt to outlaw war altogether. Launching of wars, aggressive warfare, became a breach of international law, and its prevention the duty of the international community. However, this did not effect such a great change in the institutional position of war as political, legal and lay public opinion would like to believe. Until the First World War, international law held that all states had a right to declare and wage war; but states did not exercise this right lightly, and it was mostly when they felt or at least declared themselves to be challenged or violated. The outlawing of war has not changed the fact that there are only very primitive rules, procedures and police forces for identifying and punishing the aggressor, and defensive warfare cannot therefore be forbidden in international law; also each party usually identifies the other as the aggressor and itself as the defender. War criminals have been put on trial only once — after the Second World War — and this was effected through unique laws, unique procedures and unique agencies without the subsequent acts that could make them permanent and institutional. In this case, one party, having abandoned the usual 'practice', assumed the role of aggressor on an ideological basis, thereby starting a world war. This party also lost the war with unconditional surrender.

In theory the charters of world organisations lay down the sanctions to be taken against aggressors; but the main concern of international bodies has been to avert war, or stop it through agreement or at least a cease-fire. Once a war has been halted, the mediators rarely wish to aggravate the situation by allocating blame for the aggression, or by punishing those who originally threatened or committed the aggression. With the present political structure of the world, institutional retribution is not the real way to overcome aggression, especially when the aggressor is a great power.

From this it can be seen that the institutional existence of war is not fundamentally different from the situation before the First World War, even though war has been outlawed and the international community has become more institutionalised. This becomes clear from the following observations: 1. States and nations still declare and believe themselves to be attacked or invaded before they start a war. 2. The other countries still endeavour to avert war if possible, or failing that to localise and stop it. 3. Once they have succeeded in this, the powers that be still avoid allocating blame for the aggression, let alone calling the culprit to task — for which there is still no generally valid procedure. 4. If war were to break out between all great power groups, there would be no one left to be mediator, and thus, as before, there would be no institutional arrangement to stop the war.

So war is still with us as an international institution. And although modern international law makes aggressive war a crime, there is still talk of the rules of war, rules which may, indeed, have to be elaborated because of problems caused by technical advances. The only difference between now and the past is that nuclear war threatens total destruction and, by implication, makes any thought of regulating war irrelevant. It follows, grotesquely, that 'limited' wars, fought with conventional arms, have their place. In the lee of nuclear powers which dare not risk nuclear war, there are openings for the wars or civil wars of non-nuclear powers. These are conducted not only to settle matters between the non-nuclear powers, but also as limited showdowns between the great powers themselves, who at the same time formally remain at peace with each other. These conflicts also show the nuclear powers to be impotent in certain aspects of war: they are less able than in the past to prevent the outbreak of wars amongst smaller powers, and in them they are at risk of becoming the tools of their clients. They are like tanks that can direct fire to distant points of the battlefield, but are defenceless against an infantryman sneaking up on them. And these local wars contain the danger of nuclear war, either through the spread of nuclear weapons or through the possibility that the nuclear powers may use their nuclear force.

But what can such limited wars settle? In fact, unlike in the wars of the seventeenth, eighteenth and nineteenth centuries, the situation now is such that a limited war fought with conventional weapons is hardly capable of settling anything. This is because: (i) The prolongation of a limited war poses such risks that the world organisations or non-belligerent countries tend to freeze the war at some transitional point. (ii) International public consciousness is reluctant to legalise a situation arising from war unless it results in the defeat of the aggressor. (iii) Total war, even without nuclear arms, stirs up such emotions in the populations that it becomes impossible to conclude a peace treaty confined to the original dispute. (iv) With the general acceptance of the principle of self-determination, a peace treaty is not enough to secure a country's loyalty to a new situation, or a people's loyalty to new regimes.

The following borderline cases are the only ones where it might be conceivable for war to settle anything at all: (i) If the war is very short and, excepting compulsory military service, does not become total. (ii) If the war is won by the party in the right, both by not being the aggressor and by demanding a settlement concurring with the principle of self-determination. (iii) Providing the victor does not exploit the situation beyond settlement of the original dispute — but such an unlikely case has not occurred in the period following the Second World War.

So wars have remained largely traditional in pattern and have not actually led anywhere, they only produced situations similar to those before the war, or else a mere truce. War is hardly a feasible procedure to settle contemporary state-formations and territorial adjustments; but outlawing it can only be effective if there is a central global power of absolute strength, and when there are non-military procedures to replace war.

Procedures for settling disputes by insurrection and civil disobedience

Some methods of coercion do not hold all the dangers of war, and have always had a role to play in furthering the principles of sovereignty of the people and self-determination. In particular these include insurrection, revolution and the fight for national freedom.

Insurrection was a vehicle of state-formation in the old system of international law; it foreshadowed the overthrow of the old monarchic system and, for example, it can be seen in the formation of both the Netherlands and the United States. But under the old system it was rare and it was suspect. An insurrection — which in the eighteenth century was far more costly in terms of human lives than a war — could claim recognition under the old international law only if it could show itself as similar to regular war, if it could represent a stable and orderly power capable of observing the rules of war, as in attitudes to prisoners of war, and the ability to provide distinguishing insignia or uniforms for its combatants. Today the situation is reversed. War is now far more costly than insurrection in terms of human lives, and it can only secure some respect if it contains the elements of a popular uprising – it must be seen as a freedom fight against oppressors.

Insurrection and the fight for national freedom, and the more passive civil disobedience, are now far more frequent and established means used for furthering self-determination, and the very procedure is becoming a stereotyped sequence of events. First the oppressive power tries to deal with insurrection or civil disobedience as disloyalty, and uses police and judicial action against it. This is followed by concessions, the resistance organisation being accepted eventually as a negotiating partner. The final step is an agreement with this organisation, recognising the right to self-determination, and perhaps nationhood or state-formation. A dominant power that continues treating insurgents as criminals, ruthlessly suppressing the forces of insurrection, has to face the alienation of international public opinion.

It is unlikely that a coherent system of legal rules will evolve for 'conventional' insurrection, similar to the conventions of war. This is partly because insurrections can easily trigger off wars, in the present mood of the world; also where a people in revolt are from part of the mother country, rather than a distant colony, then self-determination threatening separation is resisted by the most democratic of countries; while in less democratic countries there may be extreme retribution, even including mass deportation or genocide. So until their place can be taken by more peaceful procedures, they cannot be excluded from the possible forms of state-formation and self-determination, yet we can hardly expect insurrection and the fight for freedom to acquire accepted legislative procedures.

Civil disobedience is one such more peaceful procedure. But it demands some moral, political and legal respect from the dominant power, and the degree of this has depended upon the democratic spirit of the countries and governments concerned. For this to develop as an alternative to armed insurrection it is necessary for international police action, great power agreement, minority rights and impartial procedures to develop as well.

The problem of an international police force

The necessity for an international police force was first seen with the emergence of the global organisations after the two World Wars. But even before this, from the time of the Congress of Vienna, the great powers of the European community did occasionally act together in a manner suggesting police action. The Holy Alliance – from which Britain stayed aloof — took such actions, but they were reactionary in their aims and earned themselves a bad name. Similarly, the common actions taken against China and the Latin American debtors at the end of the nineteenth century produced nothing positive towards the preservation of peace or the solving of questions of state-formation or territorial adjustments. But the Anglo-Franco-Russian intervention in the Greek War of Independence, in which the two great Central European powers took no part, did help a nation aiming at self-determination and so helped towards the solution of a grave problem. And the common police action by the great powers in, for example, Crete and Macedonia, in the context of the dissolution of the Ottoman Empire at the beginning of this century, contributed to the lessening of administrative pressures on the subjugated nations and paved the way for their self-determination. After the two World Wars police action may be seen in several joint measures taken by the victors to implement interim decisions. All these measures were joint actions by all or several great powers, and powers not taking part were still willing to recognise them either openly or tacitly.

The question of an international force became more pressing after the World Wars, as then wars of aggression were outlawed and resolutions by world organisations needed force behind them. The Charter of the United Nations refers to armed forces in the context of settling issues brought before the Security Council, and also to a Staff Committee to direct the operations of these forces, the committee consisting of delegates of the five permanent members of the Security Council. So an international police force can and should be based, in accordance with the structure of the international community, on agreement between the great powers and on the weight of their military strength — similarly, in fact, to the previous and less institutionalised police actions of the great powers. However, the Staff Committee as laid down in the Charter has never yet functioned, nor has such a police force been used. But on at least two occasions United Nations police forces have been used in ways not stipulated in the Charter.

In practice, the Charter does not allow the use of a police force against one of the great powers. This is because although a country directly involved in a dispute is not normally allowed to vote, the rule does not apply to one of the great powers when a resolution in favour of sanctions is put before the Council. In the case of Korea, where the Soviet Union was not directly involved and refrained from using her veto for other reasons, the resolution was carried regardless of her wishes. In such circumstances, international police action would not serve the cause of peace.

For successful international police action, agreement is needed both to get greater military power and because some agreement between great powers, who may otherwise have opposing interests and systems, can alone give effect to international considerations, principles and practice.

This is the key to success for the cause of peace and the solution of problems. If the great powers take police action against each other, there is little guarantee that the action will not become the vehicle for some sort of great power policy and thus be very similar to ordinary war. Only if one of the great powers were to become aggressive, destructive and paranoid to a Hitlerian degree, could armed action against it possibly claim the character of international police action.

International police forces have been used following United Nations resolutions based on great power agreement; but the forces used have been military units provided by more or less neutral countries, not a combination of the armies of the great powers. This is not the force provided for by the Charter, but it is consistent with its spirit and it is creditably international. With the present structure of the international community, such a police force can be effective only up to a point. Its role is to occupy disputed areas, provide an international observation service and establish demilitarised zones, while perhaps calming down civil hostilities — it is not to overwhelm an aggressor or settle disputes. Recently there have been several examples of this kind of intervention, and they have been neither total successes nor total failures. Their success has depended on the extent to which they can remain independent of the political and ideological controversies of the great powers. If this can be ensured then they should intervene more boldly.

So the situation is this: an international police force whose action is but an expression of great power controversy may be effective, but its peacemaking capacity is confined to preventing extreme forces aiming at world destruction. The other kind of international police force, acting as an international organisation and under international control, may occasionally be of use in relieving tensions, but its ultimate effectiveness is limited. Because of the lack of great power agreement we have not yet seen.the kind of police envisaged in the United Nations Charter — a police force provided jointly and in concord by the great powers, which is the only form that could secure both a high degree of efficiency and the effective promotion of international considerations. So an international force is not in itself the answer to the preservation of world peace and the settling of problems — unless it is an international institution depending on the concord of the great powers. So now we must look at the present, non-violent procedures and, first among them, the institutions of international agreement.

The deadlock of international negotiations

Today the only practical alternative to settlement by war, for territorial and other political disputes is international negotiation leading to a treaty. It is vital for the international community that the procedures for this should be well established and work easily — but they are far from that.

The modern techniques of negotiation were evolved under the European monarchic-feudal system, in the seventeenth century after the wars of religion, in the Treaty of Westphalia. It helped that negotiations were conducted between parties who spoke much the same political language (not because they were all sovereigns or overlords; class allegiance was not the main factor). The negotiations were between parties brought up in the ideological confrontation of the religious wars, and they were inclined to misinterpret each other's intentions monstrously. This had to be overcome if negotiations were to proceed — and the modern European technique of international negotiation to begin to evolve. It was a hard, slow process. The negotiations preceding the peace treaty were burdened by mistrust, suspicion, formalism, quibbles over prestige and rank: it was impossible to agree on the order of entry into the conference room, so the meeting had to be held in a round hall with enough doors for all the delegates to enter at the same time. However, the evolution of the process of negotiation continued through the eighteenth century, reaching its zenith at the Congress of Vienna, when the aristocratic culture was already in decline. Characteristics of this technique of negotiation were:

(i) There were a few, uncomplicated and expedient formalities that were taken seriously and with mutual courtesy.

(ii) The negotiations were conducted privately and in a confidential atmosphere, without being paralysed by the general air of playing to the gallery — but this is not to say that all was jealously guarded secrecy.

(iii) Negotiations remained within the bounds of reality. Though the parties might use political cunning and even lies, they showed a healthy respect for unquestionable facts and did not negotiate from positions of apparent lies or the ostentatious reiteration of conditions known to be unacceptable.

(iv) The parties showed a regard for their respective strengths, without constantly and rudely drawing attention to this.

(v) They were aware of the balancing factors in preserving peace, and if the balance were upset they would try to restore it.

(vi) They did not try to annihilate each other, but only to follow the advantages of the situation.

(vii) In times of peace there was no overt hatred of each other, no cold war.

(viii) Monarchic-feudal legitimacy was a common basis of principle.

All these together created a means of negotiation that was flexible and that showed regard for facts and power and for forms and principles — which all helped in the concluding of treaties.

For this refined method of negotiation to have continued after the collapse of monarchic-feudal legitimacy at the end of the First World War, the new principle of self-determination would have had to replace the old system, and there would have had to have been a measure of solidarity amongst the self-governing peoples similar to that which had existed between the monarchies. But neither developed. The characteristic procedures and practicalities of self-determination had not been evolved; and besides, the peace negotiations following the First World War demonstrated some people calling others to task, rather than solidarity between negotiators. So the new community, based on the solidarity of peoples, did not materialise; and the changes in the technique of international relations that were to satisfy demands of the public for a new democratic international community proved to be futile.

One of these changes was the replacing of secret diplomacy by open negotiation. Public feeling blamed secret diplomacy for the wars – secret military agreements, and agreements for aims of imperialistic expansionism and so its removal was laid down as a prerequisite of democracy. But in fact secret diplomacy was adaptable to good and bad purposes, and it was to some extent unrealistic and impracticable to make negotiations public – as with the demand for treaties to be made public in a democracy based on popular representation. It is applicable to debates on principles of science or of public life, but impossible when mutual concessions are necessary for practical transactions.

The other unprecedented change was the institutionalising of international relations within a framework of organisations aiming at universality – such as the League of Nations and then the United Nations. These bodies came near to giving permanence to international discussions which previously were confined to exceptional conferences or exchange of messages. But these changes were not enough to compensate for the lack of conceptual and practical clarification of basic principles, and the need for solidarity among nations. As it was, the former smooth negotiating techniques could survive in some degree among the highly stable bourgeois democracies only, while outside their circle international relations became swamped by controversies – controversies between the 'haves' who had conceived the peace treaties, and the 'have nots' dissatisfied with them and subsequently drifting towards fascism. Also international relations became contaminated by controversy between the capitalist-liberal and the socialist-communist states, both sides claiming to have inherited the principle of freedom. Finally, the differences between the former European-American international community and the newly independent communities known collectively as the Third World also adversely influenced relations.

We may describe the present spirit and technique of international regulations as follows:

(i) Formalities have become hollow or uncertain, combining empty and stiff politeness with impulsive or deliberate rudeness and sarcasm. There is constant risk that the entire negotiation will founder in childish squabbles over procedure or prestige – such as the question of the shape of the conference table. This puts the technique of international negotiations back to the stage it had reached in the seventeenth century.

(ii) In response to the allegedly democratic demand for open negotiation there is now a sort of semi- and pseudo-public framework for discussions. In this theatre the negotiators enact roles for a presumed or real domestic or international audience, which makes the atmosphere of the discussions particularly artificial, hypocritical, mendacious and lifeless. It also influences the real talks which continue to be conducted in private.

(iii) Unquestionable facts are not respected, and there are no impartial forums. Statements will be stubbornly repeated regardless of their factual truth and insisted upon for reasons of prestige or politics. The political notion that lies are the chief weapons of politics is perverted so that even the most transparent of lies are given the status of political arguments.

(iv) Confused mutual understanding of real power relationships – resulting largely from the impotence of the great powers in war situations, while the lesser powers have more freedom of action – has created an unrealistic basis of negotiations in which the real balance of power has no bearing.

(v) The wish to annihilate the adversary morally, politically, ideologically, socially, even physically, after the pattern of the life-and-death struggle of the Second World War, makes negotiations a series of unconditional demands, thereby seriously prejudicing their success from the outset.

(vi) There is no agreement over common basic principle, above all self-determination and its practical application. The insistence on common international principles (self-determination, independence, territorial integrity, non-interference with domestic affairs) is purely formal and riddled with differing interpretations, coupled with an evasion of impartial procedures which might clarify the principles.

(vii) An attitude of ideological infallibility has become prevalent at the negotiating table, rather than a sober policy based on respect for agreed basic principles. Discussions become moral, self-righteous exhortations to the opposing party, with the result that negotiations are regarded as resounding victories for the cause of good, rather than realistic compromises.

This deterioration in the atmosphere of negotiation has appeared at a time when the absurdity of war shows negotiation to be the only feasible solution. Neither party has the courage to negotiate; but nor are they willing to take the blame for refusal to negotiate. This sometimes results in the grotesque, formalistic and unrealistic dragging out of discussions, with such a low percentage of success relative to the work put in as to suggest that the parties are virtually unable to negotiate. This is how the apparatus of international contacts works today. It is an outwardly cumbersome organisation, inwardly poisoned by distrust and unrealistically bloated in size. If we consider the main issues that affect the cause of world peace, this procedure is exceedingly inefficient compared with the money, time and expertise invested in it.

However, despite these symptoms of the utter impossibility of international understanding, inter-state negotiations take place continuously, on a conveyor-belt as it were, and the number of agreements concluded between vastly different political and economic systems far exceeds the number of treaties made in earlier times. And, of course, the intensity of international traffic and contacts has not ceased to grow. But the negotiations and treaties that we are concerned with are only those that have to do with the basic question of peace and international stability – questions relating to state-formation, territorial and other political issues: the only questions of any consequence in the international community – and it is these that have been so unsuccessful or produced such mediocre returns during the past few decades. When occasionally there have been tangible results, this has been because, despite all the difficulties and the contrary declarations of the negotiating parties, the facts have forced the parties to use the confidential techniques of the past, based on sober mutual concessions and aimed at stable balance rather than mutual annihilation.

The weakening of international treaties as a source of legitimacy

There is another reason for uncertainty of the stabilising significance of such international treaties where the social organisations have adopted democratic basic principles; this is regardless of the degree of apparent success of the negotiations. To understand this we must return to what has been said of the structure of the international community.

In international law, generally speaking, there is no difference between legal decisions at the highest level and an ordinary common law transaction. Both are to be found in the form of an international treaty. It is in this form also that exceptional changes are effected in the international constitution – in fundamental elements concerning territorial status. Likewise, a legal structure similar to a treaty serves to admit new states into the community of long-standing ones. This legal structure takes the form of two interrelated legal documents, one requesting and the other granting recognition.

How can a treaty be open to alterations in principle and in form while remaining a stabilising instrument of the international constitution in those areas regarded as unchangeable, i.e. existing states and their territorial status? In the past there were two factors that made this possible. One was the tacit convention between sovereigns that accepted war as an instrument of divine justice – so changes brought about by peace treaties or by diplomatic negotiation were considered final. The other was that European sovereigns under monarchic-feudal law were free to dispose of the loyalty of their subjects, and were also free to transfer this loyalty to others. Thus any situation involving an exchange of territory became legitimate almost immediately, and was faithfully observed by both sovereigns and subjects.

There was only one occasion involving territorial exchange between the Treaty of Westphalia and the French Revolution when more than one war and one peace treaty had to be negotiated. This was over the annexation of Silesia from Austria by Prussia, and it can be explained by the fact that the Prussian claims on Silesia lacked any dynastic foundation. Then there was the Napoleonic chapter, the capricious territorial changes of which were to be revoked by the Congress of Vienna; and there was the partition of Poland which, tragically, was not revoked. After the Congress of Vienna the old system was temporarily revived, with territorial treaties being accepted and faithfully executed. But the march of internal democratisation and, parallel to it, the growing international prevalence of the principle of self-determination, increased the problems of state-formation and territorial adjustments made through treaties without consulting the peoples concerned. The annexation of Alsace and Lorraine, sanctioned by the Frankfurt Peace Treaty, was the first contractual territorial transfer that was not followed by a change in the loyalty of the population. Similar situations were created by the territorial changes which followed the Berlin Congress, the two Balkan Wars and the First World War, though, considered as a whole, they were effected with an eye to the principle of self-determination. However, the actual frontiers were drawn up by conventional international treaties that reflected both great power politics and local balances of power; and as a result, by 1919 there were fifteen to twenty peripheral areas in Central and Eastern Europe where the populations were transferred to a state that did not command their loyalty, since it failed to satisfy their will to self-determination and national aspirations. These debatable areas were reduced to half their number after the Second World War, with new fronter adjustments, resettlement and population exchange schemes; but similar cases were to emerge among the new Asian and African states. The widely differing developments of formation and governmental stability in the new states were to show which would later be stabilised and which would cause problems and create danger spots.

For all the increasing inability to legitimise territorial changes and to effect transfer of loyalty of populations, if a treaty fails to comply with the principle of self-determination there is no procedure for invalidating it in international law, and there will not be for some time to come.

There are many sufficiently stable states with frontiers originally fixed by treaties. Some have been stabilised by time, some by a fair compromise as the basic for the treaty, some by referendum. There are stable contractual situations that were created by order of higher international bodies, world organisations, even if the motives were simply political expedience; others have gained their stability through having a government with the courage to give the country's minorities realistic civil, political and minority rights, even though their loyalty must remain incomplete. In all these cases treaties have given some degree of stabilisation.

But today no manner of bilateral agreement involving territorial change has any chance of securing the loyalty of the populations concerned unless it is in full accord with the demands for self-determination or, where there are conflicting demands, unless it is based on a valid and impartial decision. And we must be aware of this if the factors endangering peace are to be eliminated.

An example that shows the irrelevance of sanction by an international treaty is in the political status of Germany following the Potsdam negotiations that were never followed by a proper peace treaty. This has resulted in several kinds of tension; but the legitimising effect of the situation is no greater or less than that of the Versailles Treaty.

The territorial and political transactions which used to play so important a role in averting war and stabilising peace treaties in monarchic Europe, between the eighteenth century and the Congress of Vienna, are virtually extinct; and the swapping of populations without consulting them has become a classic example of the anti-democratic behaviour of monarchies. But the weakening of the effectiveness of international treaties can be seen here also, in that no alternative modern method has been devised combining observance of the principle of self-determination with the peace-keeping and stabilising functions of territorial transfers and reciprocal concessions.

The weakening of recognition and diplomatic relations as a source of legitimacy

Under the old international law, a sufficiently stable and independent state-formation would always, sooner or later, gain recognition from the rest of the community, and even in time from the state at whose expense it was formed. But today, as a result of political and ideological rifts in the international community, recognition and diplomatic relations have become the capriciously wielded weapons of international political differences, emotional impulses or political tactics. Their stabilising function, like that of the international treaty, has greatly weakened.

At first sight the connection between this development and the advance of self-determination may not be apparent, but it should be noticed how often recognition is withheld chiefly on the grounds that the country or territory concerned has no real independence or self-determination – and these arguments reflect a view that is becoming internationally prevalent.

While the significance of the international treaty, of recognition and diplomatic relations has decreased, a new form of sanctioning of state-formations has evolved – though it does not essentially alter the situation. This new form is in the Security Council's granting of membership to the United Nations, and perhaps when the United Nations has become fully universal this form of sanction may completely replace recognition by individual countries. The Security Council's authority over the eventual independence of trusteeship territories is another, though temporary, role which it has in the sanctioning of state-formations and frontiers. Both these contain elements of impartial decision-making by experts, and they provide additional security against blatant tyranny; but they are still expressions of political compromise based on short-term expediency. The powers which make the decisions consider their own interests first, and only then examine the immediate administrative feasibility of the new state. Minimal attention is paid as to whether the new formations are based on true self-determination and contain the conditions or at least the prospect of nation-formation. So such decisions will hardly have the authority, the capability of providing legitimacy and inspiring loyalty to the new situation that the former international treaties and recognition had.

The situation, then, is that the weight of international treaties and recognition has considerably decreased, while the weight of the Security Council's decisions has not become sufficient to give the legitimacy to new state-formations and territorial changes that would include acceptance by the populations concerned. So these legal instruments can hardly continue to be the only vehicles for stable state-formation and territorial change.

The minority status and territorial autonomies

The great powers have, in fact, been concerned about this weakening of the legitimising effect of treaties – even though it is their own short-term interests that have often brought it about.

The Congress of Berlin – a face-saving gesture towards the disintegrating Ottoman Empire – left in the Balkans a considerable non-Turkish population under Ottoman rule, and European powers were later obliged to intervene for minority rights and territorial autonomy in Macedonia and Crete. Because of this, after the First World War the great powers drew up binding minority guarantees for the Eastern European countries, some of which included territorial autonomy. But the powers concerned resented these guarantees and did not carry out the obligations willingly, while the minorities in question did not feel them sufficient reason for any shift of loyalty. The great tensions caused by these arrangements helped Hitler to power, and triggered off the Second World War. The new settlement after 1945 did not include this system of minority status, but it had not been the guarantees themselves that he led to such disastrous developments – rather it had been the fact that they had failed to achieve the expected quick transfer of loyalties.

However, such statutes could still play a modest part today. An arrangement based on territorial autonomy could fill the gap in procedure for state-formation and territorial change – this in a system where coercion is outdated or dangerous, and peaceful international forums are confronted with the demand for territorial stability, characteristic of the international community. In a democratic regime, such an arrangement based on minority rights might command suitable behaviour from the minority, if not patriotic enthusiasm. Such minority status, or territorial autonomy, may be created through a governmental decision within the state, through legislation, or through constitutional amendment. At the same time they may be laid down in a bilateral agreement between two countries, or in an undertaking in a wider international forum. Where a serious, responsible power is concerned, a governmental or other domestic decision is enough; but pledges made by irresponsible governments before an international forum are of little consequence. Whatever the form they take – and this includes that of domestic legal provisions – they are part of the balance of the international community.

This, of course, does not apply where the minority consists of scattered immigrants and seeks assimilation, or where territorial self-government simply meets the demand for local administration. But it applies where territorial autonomy or minority guarantees are seen as the answers to nationality problems, as functions of the principle of self-determination. It is desirable that the solutions should be supported by the concord of the great powers as keepers of the international balance, and – for procedural reasons – by an impartial forum. In the long run it may seem best for minority rights and, where necessary, for territorial autonomies, to be incorporated as binding obligations in international law. But in the shorter term it could be useful to revive the post-First World War interest in minority statues so that newly formed states . whose domestic administration is not yet stable, and countries receiving international aid, should – among other duties to be discussed – undertake to secure minority rights as part of the conditions of recognition, membership or aid.

For these institutionalised arrangements to function properly, a delicate balance must be reached in the psychological approach of the countries concerned. A state that contains minorities must sense the weight of the principle of self-determination and be aware that the primary loyalty of these minorities is not to itself; and it must refrain from any attempt to force shows of patriotism from the minorities, and from any steps to break their primary national loyalty. And despite these shared loyalties, the state must be prepared to secure equal civil rights for the minorities, along with the additional minority rights due to them. At the same time the minorities must know that the price for non-discrimination and realistic rights lies in correct behaviour and a measure of civil loyalty; and this same correctness must be reflected in the behaviour of a neighbouring country with ethnic links with the minority concerned.

After the First World War the view was often held that the obligations stipulated in peace treaties were the outside concern of only the great powers or the League of Nations, and otherwise were purely domestic matters not to be questioned by neighbours racially related to the minorities concerned. But this is hollow formalism. An elementary prerequisite of the proper functioning of minority rights and territorial self-governments – and of international balance in this respect – is that the neighbouring racially related country should adopt an attitude of co-operation, rather than a strict denial of any interests in the fate of the minority concerned; there have recently been a number of realistic bilateral negotiations between states with minorities and their interested neighbours.

In these matters the majority in the state has to take the greater initiative. A state will gain a minority's loyalty according to its courage to grant minority rights or territorial autonomy, and it must be aware that such an attitude may be rewarded as much by stabilisation and a strengthening of the minority's civil loyalty as by increased separatism. The state must also be aware that the more these rights are denied the stronger the possibility that a minority movement will become a separatist one. In other words the cause of a separatist movement is never in the granting of minority status or territorial self-government, but in the dynamism of nation-formation which is only fomented by oppression. It may happen that a state of balance will not be achieved, either because of the authority's suspicion and lack of generosity, or because of the separatist minority's lack of even limited civil loyalty. It is impossible to give a general rule as to when these solutions will succeed, but certain features of the situation help us to deduce their chances. For instance, we may assume with reasonable confidence that the territorial autonomy of the Aaland and Faroe Islands or the Val d'Aosta promises stable solutions to the problems concerned, while this seems more doubtful in Alto-Adige or Northern Ireland.

So, minority guarantees or territorial self-government aimed at solving questions of nationality may be justified by historical links, by the smallness or territorial isolation of the minorities or, above all, by the reluctance of the majority power to give up the territory concerned. But even when the solutions prove successful, in most cases they are only substitutes for the full application of the principle of self-determination.

Resettlement of populations

It is paradoxical that population resettlement and exchange is contrary to the principle of self-determination from which it is derived. The practice of resettlement and exchange is based on the realisation that, since self-determination is the prevalent concept, there is little chance of gaining the loyalty of a nationally alien population to a state that has acquired the territory on which they live – and there is no way of quickly gaining this loyalty. This is why the practice of resettlement and exchange has been used in the twentieth century.

The first such project, the Graeco-Turkish population exchange, involved unilateral mass deportation which later became mutual exchange sanctioned further by a peace treaty. Notwithstanding the numerical imbalance of the exchange, it speedily relieved tensions and led to acceptance of the new situation it helped to bring about. This was made easier for the Greeks, as they made room for their refugees from Asia Minor at the expense of their own Macedonian and Bulgarian minorities.

During the Second World War, Hitler tried quite wide-scale resettlement of distant German minorities in his empire; and his expansionist ideas also included monstrous deportations covering entire peoples and virtually amounting to genocide. Some of these ideas were actually carried out while others mercifully remained mere projects. After the collapse of the Third Reich, mass deportation was employed on a smaller scale against the Germans themselves – a situation that unexpectedly proved stable because these ten million Germans were almost immediately caught up by an unprecedented economic boom.

A third example is more alarming: the removal of Arabs from territories earmarked for Israeli national resettlement. When this started in 1948-9, the first waves were more or less counterbalanced by some Arab countries deporting their own Jewish minorities to Israel, though not in quite the same numbers. Even quite recently Arab refugee camps contained much of the residue of the 1949 refugees, partly due to the shaky economies of the recipient countries, partly because the Arab States, as a matter of political principle, never accepted the situation; and it was partly due to the fact that the great powers unfortunately did not consider it their collective duty to relieve such sufferings or to find a comprehensive solution to the causes. Recent developments have only aggravated the situation.

So resettlement has, on occasion, had a stabilising effect, but it can equally create extremely dangerous situations, and it can be fatal from the standpoint of long-term international territorial legitimacy and stability: for example, a country could find it desirable to carry out disproportionate or unguaranteed deportation in order to stabilise territorial change achieved through short-term power superiority. If this practice were to become widespread, it would destroy the last remaining and accepted basis of territorial legitimacy – the right of peoples to be masters of their own territory. Beyond this we would reach a moral and political void which would be a counterpart to the physical void through which nuclear warfare threatens mankind.

Yet a mutual population exchange can have its place if it is carried out under international control and guarantees, and is employed only as an exceptional procedure for an explosive situation. Those so far undertaken were largely in the sanctioning of *de facto* exchanges already executed or in progress, but still the question must arise whether such a population exchange should be compulsory or voluntary. Responsible statesmen naturally enough abhor compulsory exchanges as inhumane and profoundly in contradiction with the right to self-determination; but voluntary resettlement is essentially ineffectual. Between the two there is the possibility of mutual resettlement, internationally organised and encouraged through international financial aid, and this may best serve to reach its goal. But this is again dependent on concord among the great powers, an international police force, and an impartial procedure to formulate conditions.

The problem of plebiscites

From war to international treaties, the procedures so far discussed are mostly institutions or phenomena of the old international community. Insurrection, minority statutes, population resettlement are all in some way connected with self-determination – the first directly, the second as a substitute, the third paradoxically; but none of them derives from the need to practise self-determination or can be called its peaceful procedure. The only procedure with any such claim is the plebiscite, derived as it is from the principle of self-determination, and able to inherit the functions of the old dynastic treaty and diplomatic recognition in the field of state-formation, territorial adjustment and transfer of loyalty. Renan in defining the principle of self-determination said that the nation is a constant referendum. In the eyes of modern public opinion a fairly conducted referendum, with questions relevant to the reality and the essence of the problem, possesses the authority to close a problem, legitimise a situation and command loyalty to the decision.

A plebiscite, as a simpler institution for sanctioning territorial change, cannot alone replace the international treaty since a plebiscite is far more complex and vulnerable than a treaty. This is shown by the need for guarantees to ensure the fairness of a referendum.

First of all, some authority must define the problem and how the question should be formulated, which requires caution, political judgement and good faith. If the questions are formulated in bad faith, then self-determination and the smooth process of nation-formation may be impeded. For peoples still in the early stages of democracy, it is possible to sidetrack the whole process of a referendum into advocacy of short-term economic interests, political emotions, and likes and dislikes of the present authority – generally into exploitation by demagogues. Social scientists seriously analyse the opportunities for manipulation in the way the questions are put, their order and the conditions for further rounds of referenda. Unbiased decisions are required in all these questions if the credit of the plebiscite is to be upheld. And there are situations in which a referendum is superfluous when the will for nation-formation clearly complies with certain outward criteria – for example, long-established historic frontiers; linguistic or ethnic lines, and so on. These are situations in which a referendum would not reveal new facts, in which the available statistical and other data give sufficient grounds for a correct decision, always provided that there is an objective and impartial forum to guarantee that avoiding a referendum does not mean the avoidance of self-determination. It is also necessary to evaluate the territorial equivalent of contradictory results and to establish certain basic criteria. Finally, referenda must be conducted in the presence of some kind of police and of observers, who should be international and neutral rather than delegated by the great powers.

The vulnerability of the plebiscite is well illustrated in its history. The first plebiscites of international significance took place in Europe in the mid-nineteenth century, largely as a consequence of Napoleon III's policy for national independence. Even if they corresponded with popular will and the trends of nation-formation, they lacked guarantees of fairness; and Napoleon III and his entourage were well aware that referenda can be easily manipulated. Following the First World War, the referenda ordered by the peace treaties were conducted more fairly, but they were also only incidental and prescribed as results of local uprisings and occasional bargains. However, their effect in stabilising and legitimising the new situations turned out to be far stronger than the frontiers drawn by mere superiority of power. Denmark paid great tribute to the principle of self-determination when she refused to accept the parts of Schleswig that did not show a desire, through plebiscite, to belong to her – Schleswig being a territory with a mixed population of Danes and Germans and strong historical ties with Denmark. These referenda were all conducted under the supervision of largely impartial, *ad hoc* commissions.

The referendum conducted in the Saar was the most significant episode of plebiscite during the inter-war period in that it showed the vulnerability of the process. The Western countries refrained from simply annexing this German-populated land to France after the war, which formed a token of respect for the principle of self-determination and for responsible international behaviour. But the referendum of fifteen years later, though fairly conducted, was a most paradoxical application of the procedure. It so happened that the whole German nation was seized with mass hysteria, partly on account of the obstacles in the way of nation-formation and self-determination. So another 300,000 of its fellow nationals voted to join this gangsters' regime, thus giving the government a resounding success in foreign politics, even though it was government based on tyranny, having abolished all freedom and self-determination. This episode does not make the importance and usefulness of the plebiscite any the less. But it shows that it is vulnerable, and that only a system of impartial procedures far more comprehensive than exists at present can save the plebiscite from the dangers that can destroy its usefulness.

After the Second World War there were several plebiscites promulgated in resolutions of the U.N. for agreements between colonial powers and national liberation movements, and for colonial powers intending to end their colonial rule. The referenda were mostly fair in their form, but often they covered arbitary units rather than the total situation, and the questions were poorly formulated, sometimes even in bad faith. On occasion the alternative most favoured by the population was simply omitted; on other occasions the referendum left it possible for short-term interests, emotions, intimidation or political immaturity to divert the voters' attention from fundamental questions. This sometimes resulted in there being no possibility of self-determination for the population, or produced an answer which impeded or halted the process of nation-formation or stabilisation rather than enhancing them.

So, though the method of plebiscite has recently spread and has become more impartial, the practice has shown two major shortcomings that have greatly reduced or even obliterated its effectiveness. One is that the impartial procedure is hardly ever concerned with the basic issue: the formulation of the questions. At best it is usually confined to the actual conduct of the referendum and perhaps to interpretation of the result and the decisions following it. The other shortcoming is that the plebiscite commissions which have been employed have never been in institutionalised consultation with each other, and so they have not evolved coherent procedure and concepts from their experience, from the continuous development of processes employed by the various commissions, and they have not effected any progress towards self-determination. This is why the plebiscite is to this day practised only occasionally and subject to political considerations. This can only be remedied if the plebiscite as a procedure can become institutionalised as part of a system of impartial international arbitration. So none of the present international procedures for settling problems of state-formation, territorial settlements and other political issues function adequately, even by modest standards.'

The institutional functioning of the concert of great powers and impartial international arbitration

We have seen that neither insurrection nor war can become vehicles for successful international settlements – and so it is vital that they be replaced by an international police force and international negotiations as feasible institutions, or that they become feasible and institutional through the concord of great powers. We have seen, too, that the international treaty has ceased to be a vehicle for the transfer of the loyalty of populations, and so new procedures and institutions are needed that are able to secure harmony between state frontiers and popular loyalties. The procedures that have hitherto been evolved – be they plebiscite, minority statutes or population resettlement – can only function successfully if there are coherent institutions of impartial international arbitration to develop consistency in the application of the basic principles of the international community, above all self-determination.

The old system of international law is not enough to give substance to the basic principles of the modern international community. It drew no distinction between the functions of great power agreement and summit level decision, which together constituted the assembly of great powers; a state of affairs that was permitted because the joint will of sovereigns was the formal source of legality and was able to command the loyalty of the people. Democratic principles, in contrast, demand a more differentiated system under which the function of great power agreement is divorced from impartial arbitration. On the surface, it would seem that such a differentiation has come about: modern international law recognises the Security Council as an institutional form of great power agreement; and it recognises the International Court of Justice and other specialist international courts as the agencies for impartial arbitration. However, experience shows that the Security Council functions inadequately, while the functioning of the international courts is irrelevant to the vital questions of war and peace, state-formation and territorial dispute. The question is: why?

[10]

The Working of the Concert of Great Powers Today and Inadequacy of Institutions and Procedures

The concert of great powers in the past and present

Although democratic principles require perhaps more differentiated procedures than were needed in the old monarchic system, there is still need for institutions of concord among great powers. In order to examine why these institutions do not function adequately, we will first look at the form and rules of the old international community of European monarchies.

The concept of great powers is a product of the Congress of Vienna. Prior to that the differences between strong and weak countries had, of course, been felt, but the formal distinction between states still reflected medieval categories (the order of rank among the kingdoms, feudal relations). During the Congress of Vienna the four victorious countries began to negotiate privately with each other. France as a strong power protested against this, as did less significant countries as allies. France's protest was successful; that of the allies was overruled. Thus it became routine that the five major powers would conduct separate negotiations over the more important and general issues, while the minor powers would only be consulted in matters that immediately concerned them.

Up to the outbreak of the First World War the so-called European concert — i.e. great power agreement — was seen in the form of congresses, conferences or diplomatic exchanges. The main fields of their deliberations involved the preservation of peace through negotiation, the re-establishment of balance and of peace negotiations following major European wars, and decisions over exceptional territorial changes and state-formations, and also matters such as spheres of interest and maritime routes; besides, the ensemble of great powers created several conventions for developing or amending rules concerned with peace and war, and they made decisions over questions of general or humanitarian interest. In brief, the primary function of the great power concert was to amend the international constitution, particularly as manifested in the ensemble of states and the territorial *status quo*. The main features of this were the resolutions of the Congress of Vienna in 1815, the London Protocol and Conference of 1830 giving independence to Belgium and Greece, the 1856 ,Congress of Paris concluding the Crimean War, and the 1878 Congress of Berlin concluding the Russo-Turkish war.

The great powers were thus seen to serve as legislative or constitutional bodies of international law whose resolutions affected the entire international community – but this was never institutionalised, and there was no source of international law to list the great powers or to say that any of their resolutions was binding for any other country which did not accept it in the form of an international treaty. In other words the great power concert had no institutional agencies and procedures.

But the legal regulation of a social structure is only one aspect of its *de facto* functioning. Customary patterns of behaviour, whether legally regulated or not, are at least as important: an institution is perfectly able to function on the basis of traditional conventions and in the absence of formal legal regulation, but the reverse is not true. The European concert of powers was not codified by law, but it had its established habits and tacit conventions. These were far less articulated than the conventions of the British parliament, for example, but we will try to draw their outlines.

(i) The technique of international negotiation described in the previous chapter was used in the main by the ensemble of great powers. This technique was relatively smooth and, not overburdened with formal codes, it politely respected the established ones. Negotiations were conducted confidentially and in private, without play-acting and intransigence for the benefit of the public. There was respect for realities, existing power relations and balances; and the negotiators never tried to destroy each other, or questioned the common ground of monarchic-feudal legitimacy.

(ii) The great powers generally negotiated and reached decisions to the exclusion of the smaller countries, who were only invited to see the treaties once they had been concluded. Occasionally they would allow a small country with momentary importance to take part, as in the case with Sardinia at the 1856 Paris Congress, and Spain in 1912 at the Congress of Algeciras. But they never allowed their negotiations to become mass meetings of the smaller countries.

(iii) Despite this, the agreements reached were never seen in the light of great power resolutions, but always in the classic form of international treaties valid also for the smaller countries. In practice pressures, even coercion, were brought to bear, as with victors in peace treaties after war – but the great powers always went out of their way to keep this coercion within bounds; even clear dictates were never shown in their true nature but were couched in polite diplomatic terms.

(iv) Although the great power concert consisted of the most powerful, it contained a good balance that always helped in curbing the stronger and more victorious; and the congresses as a rule produced more restrained and conciliatory agreements and peace treaties than peace negotiations conducted between two parties alone.

(v) The concept of balance was quite important in the system of mutual concessions, compensations and transactions. The more responsible statesmen were inclined to regard the concept of balance as a constant process of watching, listing, counterbalancing and compensating all factors tending to upset the general balance, rather than as an automatic device of equilibrium or a title to gain; whereas the more aggressive powers would immediately claim compensation if another power gained strength or territory to their detriment.

(vi) The great powers, especially round the conference table, were aware that they had to reach an agreement, that they could not go home without one, that both politically and morally they owed it to themselves and to the world, and that failure to agree meant the threat of war.

(vii) Whatever was decided would be carried out as a matter of course. It was not customary to pass resolutions that were mere declarations of intent, and it was clearly indicated by means of reservations or protests if agreement was less than full.

(viii) The solutions, happy or otherwise, were accepted with finality. When they were successful this meant a durability to be measured in centuries, while even the worst solutions would last a few decades. At the same time it was not customary to prolong provisional situations indefinitely.

These eight points are an attempt to show the contrasts with the present system, rather than a summing up of the implicit rules and conventions of the concert of great powers, nor is it suggested that they were always unfailingly and consciously observed. However, I believe that by and large these points reflect the common spirit that characterised the functioning of the great power concert.

For all this, the European great power concert was a very imperfect and primitive organisation. In the course of its hundred years' existence it averted a few wars, localised the rest, and settled the problems presented to it with more or less finality; but it could not cope with the contradictions evolving in society and, in the end, it was unable to prevent the First World War.

Following the two World Wars, the Council of the League of Nations and the Security Council of the United Nations were both meant to provide a more effectual and organised institution in place of the concert of great powers — but it now appears that they have been far less effective and energetic than the latter ever was.

Collapse of the European concert and failure of the League of Nations

The collapse of the European concert of powers came dramatically at the end of the First World War. The peace treaty at this time took place in a semi-public arena brought about by the rejection of secret diplomacy. The victorious Western powers, vitiated by the absence of the Soviet State, took the attitude of a tribunal facing a defeated Germany and her allies. The peace treaties that were concluded fell short of the unemotional bargains formerly struck by monarchs and peoples. The Treaty of Locarno was an attempt to repair the rifts so caused, but even with the re-admittance of Germany into the family of nations this was not enough to restore the smooth negotiation and political traditions of the concert of great powers, or to permit new forms of great power agreement to evolve on the basis of the democratic solidarity of peoples.

Political awareness, combined with mutual hostility and mistrust, allowed the techniques of international agreement to sink into oblivion; and that same political awareness, in an almost schizophrenic manner, pinned the highest and least realistic hopes on the new international organisation. The supreme purpose of the organisation was to be the eradication of the possibility of war, which was no longer conceivable as an international procedure but only as something endangering the whole future of mankind; and it was expected by public opinion that a supra-national organisation could do this in the same way that a centralised state could abolish civil strife between its individual citizens. Thus all the planning and political and judicial endeavours went into the creation of new institutions that would, at first glance, resemble a sovereign parliament and a central government – but the structural features of the international community did not possess the central power to run such institutions (and it does not seem likely to possess it in the foreseeable future). The structural features of the international community and the problems that threaten peace and stability require far more modest institutions than a parliament and a government, and are crying out for these.

But in the collective shock caused by the First World War the realistic solutions were thought insufficient. And it was no good suggesting then that the first task was to restore and improve the structure of concord among the great powers, while public opinion – quite rightly – alleged that the war had been caused by the policies of great powers. Equally, it was no good suggesting that, in accepting the principle of self-determination, the plebiscite and political arbitration should be institutionalised, when people remembered that international arbitration had not been called upon to avert war, even though that was the purpose of the Hague Court of Arbitration in pre-war years.

These contradictory facts resulted in the creation of the League of Nations after the First World War. Its General Assembly, which was composed of delegations from all the member states, gave the superficial impression that it was a sovereign parliament of the international community; and the Council, which was composed of those great powers that were members and a few smaller powers elected for limited periods, gave the impression, again superficial, that it was a sort of international government. In fact the League of Nations, through its organisation, composition and spirit, fell far short of what could have been achieved in preserving peace. Public opinion expected a universal and institutional peace-making organisation that would exclude war altogether; an organisation which would take the place of the old concert of powers that was only fairly effective (it was unable to exclude war), fairly universal (it was limited mainly to Europe) and not properly institutional in its peace-preserving activity. Yet the new organisation could perform rather less than the old concert of powers for the following reasons:

1. The legal framework of its procedure made effective action impossible: its Covenant stipulated that any resolution of either the General Assembly or the Council had to be unanimous to be valid – so apart from a few exceptions the vote of those parties directly concerned was required, this being in accordance with the classic rule of international law that no state can be charged with an international obligation without its own consent.

2. While the League of Nations existed the great powers were divided into the categories of bourgeois democratic, communist, and fascist states, into victors and vanquished, satisfied and dissatisfied countries, and into member states and isolationist ones. Small wonder that they had less common ground in domestic or foreign policies than at any time before or since.

3. The League of Nations was considerably less universal than the earlier concert of great powers since throughout its existence it lacked the support of one of the greatest powers in the world – the U.S.A. – and for more than half its life it failed to include another world power – the U.S.S.R. This, together with the withdrawal of the fascist states, caused a void that was increasingly filled by the medium and small powers which used the position to achieve equal status in the Council with the great powers. So when the League of Nations had to face the task of preserving peace or curbing the aggressor in Europe, it had already squandered the little authority it ever had over the Far and Middle East conflicts. And the Council which at first consisted of four great and four minor powers, in the end consisted of only two great powers of Western Europe and ten medium and small powers!

It was right and necessary that the lesser powers should have been given seats in the Council. However, minor powers can only supplement, but do not replace, great powers in international institutions. Their presence was a necessary counterbalance to the anti-democratic trend towards giving the great powers authority to make binding decisions affecting the others; and their restrained and responsible participation in the Council might even have increased the responsibility shown by this body.

As a consequence of all this, the great powers lost their enthusiasm for discussing the vital world problems in the Council of the League of Nations.

This failure also happens with the United Nations Security Council when institutional, organisational, political or power considerations make it inexpedient for the Council to function as the vehicle of great power agreement. It is as if the old concert of great powers reappears, with the system of occasional great power meetings, to hammer out some solution. But the reappearance of these non-formal meetings does not mean the revival of the diplomatic, restrained and responsible conventions of the old monarchies; rather these meetings are called with the intention of circumventing the Security Council, and this makes politics increasingly formal within the organisation and increasingly irresponsible outside it.

It is not harmful for decisions made outside the world organisation to be later incorporated into its rules − as in the case of the Locarno agreements concluded outside the League of Nations, or the agreement against nuclear proliferation concluded outside the United Nations. However, it is much worse when such an extra-organisational great power convention becomes the scene of some irresponsible political bargaining and resembles a war-mongering conspiracy more than a forum of great power agreement. This sort of procedure led to Hitler's infamous pacts, in particular the Munich Agreement which trampled on both the traditions of the old European concert and the principles of the League of Nations. The Munich Agreement passed a resolution concerning a vital European question without including all the great powers; it took a decision affecting a small country that was given not even a minimal opportunity to take part in the discussions; it failed to regulate the execution of the territorial change or to guarantee it, and thus it delivered a small country to the mercy of an an aggressive great power.

So by the outbreak of the Second World War the traditional and modern agencies of great power agreement were out of action and virtually out of existence as well.

The end of the Second World War and the principles of the United Nations

The settlement following the Second World War contributed nothing to the techniques of peace-making. The peace treaties signed with Germany's former allies were less dictatorial in character than in 1918, but then this was mainly because by the end of the war those former allies were converted to the other side. And mass emotion had been so stirred up against the atrocities of Hitlerism, placing the main burden of responsibility on the Germans, that the victorious powers quite simply took over the administration of Germany. This action required far greater unanimity of the victors than the arrangements following the First World War – and as we know, this virtually ceased to exist within a few years, leading to the creation of two Germanies.

The United Nations Organisation created at the end of the war was far more successful than its predecessor and was launched on a more realistic legal basis. The elements of this basis are as follows:

1. The Security Council, in contrast to the Council of the League of Nations, passes its resolutions with a majority decision (7:4 and more recently 9:6), a majority that must include all permanent members, though in some cases – defined in a rather complicated way – members directly concerned in a dispute cannot vote.
2. Member states undertake to regard resolutions passed by the Security Council as binding on themselves.
3. The General Assembly of the United Nations can only make recommendations and must not discuss issues currently before the Security Council.

By and large, the regulations are well suited to the structure of the international community. But there are many who criticise the power of veto that is inherent in the rule that prescribes the unanimous consent of all permanent members of the Security Council to a resolution. It is believed that this is in effect the same obstacle to smooth functioning as the requirement of unanimity was for the League of Nations. Natural progress is seen as a move from the unanimity required of the League of Nations to the qualified majority with the right of veto of the United Nations, which should be followed by the principle of a simple majority.

This view is rooted in a misconception of the very nature of the international community, and this 'natural' progression could only be possible if the international community begins to assemble around an overwhelmingly powerful centre. While the international community continues to be a community of sovereign states, some of them great powers which are unable to dominate each other, the right of the veto will remain a prerequisite for critical political resolutions, and this is a structure that seems unlikely to change for a long time to come. In such a community a primary condition of communal will is at least a minimum of great power agreement, and without this the community cannot function and is threatened with war; without it there is neither peace nor international organisation.

The very expression 'veto' is misleading, and it does not appear in the

Charter. It suggests that there is an established communal will that cannot be followed because of the veto of a single power. But once we accept that agreement between the great powers is at the core of any international will, it is not possible to speak of international will in the absence of such agreement, and it is futile to count the votes. At the same time the representation of the lesser powers is both right and useful; but their vote cannot be substituted for the primary requisite: great power agreement. Other countries may be voted down, but the great powers must come to terms. In other words the right of veto does not mean that a single power has the right to prevent resolutions, but that it is the collective duty of the members of the Security Council, and above all its permanent members, to reach an agreement. If they fail it is not necessarily because they avail themselves of the right of veto; it may equally be because the veto was used in bad faith or irresponsibly by one or more powers, or by the majority.

In order that the right of veto will not be abused, the Charter stipulates that interested parties should not vote. However, the rule is complex, and in a serious situation it does not allow a great power with a permanent seat in the Security Council to be voted down or punished with sanctions – even less so than under the Covenant of the League of Nations. As we have seen, military sanctions against a great power would easily become a power struggle with one of the contenders fighting in U.N. police uniform. An effective counterbalance to veto by the great powers could be, in extreme cases, to allow the suspension of a country's membership – great power or otherwise – if the country becomes subject to dictatorship of Hitlerian proportions, political paranoia, racial ideology, or some other irrational insanity. This we shall see later in Chapter 11 in the context of an international political tribunal.

There is a contrasting view that condemns the stipulation that member states must undertake to observe the Security Council resolutions aimed at the peaceful settlement of disputes. This, it is argued, is premature in the evolution of the international community. Such an undertaking is, indeed, the first instance in international law where a source of law of general validity ranks higher than an international treaty, and binds states without their explicit consent. It is certainly an important development in the history of international legal rules, but in effect it is not an abandonment of previous concepts or an impractical novelty. Resolutions expressing the agreement of the great powers have always been observed through the strength of the facts; and this new type of international law is concerned with conciliation rather than with the enforcing of general rules, state-formation or territorial adjustments, even if there is a theoretical possibility of these.

Finally, the fact that the General Assembly's resolutions are merely recommendations and that it cannot discuss matters currently under consideration by the Security Council, shows that the Security Council is the prime agency of the formation of internation will, embodying as it does the agreement of the great powers.

All these rules create the conditions required for the realistic legal framework that is needed for effective operation. Added to this, the U.N. comes far nearer to world-wide universality than did the League of Nations, and so it has better prospects of becoming the organising agency of world peace. It is not the fault of the legal concepts laid down in the Charter that it has only partially justified the high expectations of it.

The tacit conventions to maintain the Security Council

More than realistic regulations are needed for great power agreement to function properly within the framework of the United Nations. In order to soften the frictions that necessarily accompany international action and the expression of community will, the modern international community needs to develop conventional habits — as with the old conventions of the European monarchies. It needs to evolve a new common spirit, understood procedural routine and conventions compatible with the spirit of its characteristics and legal regulations. If the Security Council is to have the efficacy of the old concert of powers, there are certain explicit or implicit conventions that must be part of the common conviction. These are:

1. Permanent places in the Security Council should be occupied by only those countries that are populous, economically powerful and politically stable enough to bear the burdens and responsibilities that such membership entails — and no other countries. Countries should on no account seek permanent membership of the Council for prestige reasons alone, and no puppet government that is without considerable power may be a permanent member. No shadow-governments should be given membership, as this undermines the authority and the operational ability of the Security Council; and if an altogether irresponsible government comes to power in a country, then membership rights must be suspended. In time it may become necessary to revise the register of great powers and regulate the position among them of superpowers, but it is too early to do this now.

2. The non-permanent members of the Security Council ought to represent above all those groups of medium and small powers which jointly make up a geographical unit equal to a great power; failing this they should represent groupings of real political weight, with sufficient governmental stability and ability in international mediation to add to the weight of the small countries. Membership must on no account be considered an honour to be bestowed automatically in rotation upon as many countries as possible. Non-permanent members discharge an international public service. Besides representing minor powers, their

task should be to mediate among the major powers, to promote great power agreement and to help raise it above the mere correspondence of interests to the higher levels of principles and ethics. At the same time they must not let their principles lapse into dogmatism or force their own petty interests in such a way that the great powers should turn away from the Security Council for negotiating important matters. So the non-permanent members must never exceed their own effective weight, or try to sell their votes for political advantage, or exercise prestige politics, since that is even more harmful than the prestige politics exercised by the major powers.

3. The Security Council's discussions must all concern important issues, and no others. (For this reason it is essential that the non-permanent members do not, through their behaviour, encourage the great powers to negotiate elsewhere.) But members can consult each other at a preliminary conference, for exchange of views, before passing a resolution in the Council itself — as some of the great powers have been trying to do over the Middle East. What must be avoided are discussions kept off the Council's agenda through veto or majority vote, because they concern an issue that is suspect for world peace. If this kind of situation became too frequent, the Security Council could become relegated to a secondary arena, in which case the resolutions would lose much of their authority. In other words, more than other countries, it is important that the great powers pursue policies which are responsible and of a high order; the high-level organisation of great power agreement can only function if great power policies are highly responsible — otherwise the Security Council might as well be disbanded.

4. The Security Council is an institution for settling concrete outstanding issues — it is not a public forum, it is not a place for pompous preaching or mutual abuse intended for public consumption. The duty of its members is to pass valid, fruitful and effective resolutions — it is not to vote as their 'conscience dictates' like parliamentary deputies. For this reason it seldom has to hold meetings and vote in public, and when it does it is to give valid form to existing agreements and to provide necessary information for the world public; it is not in order to show off strengths, which in any case are not always the same in public as they are in private. The right of veto exists, not to be used or misused *per se*, but simply through its existence to force the great powers to agree. The dangers inherent in the veto can be counterbalanced only by a common spirit that accepts the moral pressure to agree.

5. Only real decisions must be made in the Security Council, not mere paper agreements that serve only to conceal the absence of real decisions. It is better for resolutions to be modest and limited than

formal and verbal, ambiguous and hollow — particularly since the General Assembly is the place for resolutions containing long-term programmes of a conceptual nature. It is much better openly to admit failure to agree than to disguise the failure with pseudo-actions and declarations.

6. The Security Council's decisions must be realistic: decisions which can be executed and are intended to be. They must also reflect the Council's determination to overcome any objections, relying on the collective strength of its members. This does not mean ultimatums and threats of coercion, but it means the intention to use the full arsenal of great power pressures, and not to temporise and wait for developments to give effect to decisions or to render them unnecessary.

7. The General Assembly is a forum of public life. Its task is to issue declarations of principle, long-term guidelines and warnings. Its resolutions are in the nature of recommendations; they are not binding resolutions intended for direct execution. Votes in the General Assembly are not to be regarded as tests of strength in the world political arena and they should never be used for mere demonstrations. It is an admission of failure of great power concert if an issue that belongs to the Security Council is dragged before the General Assembly as a way of circumventing the right of veto, as a way of dealing public blows on an adversary, or of urging resolutions which everybody knows in advance will be ineffectual.

These are the conventions that are needed for the Security Council to be an effective agency of great power agreement and of world peace. The old concert of powers achieved its results through observing such conventions, though more primitive ones. The results did not satisfy the world, but they can be remembered as a minimum standard for the far more institutionalised and more organised world organisations of today. There is no sign that a consistent system of such conventions has been observed, or that it has evolved to become the common conviction, although on some occasions some of these, or similar principles, have affected the operations of the Security Council, one or two being so fundamental that they are hard to reject.

In many respects a diametrically opposite routine has been established. One characteristic of this is that the affairs of the great powers do not reach the Security Council, and this turns the Council into a secondary political forum. Both the General Assembly and the Security Council have been used as battlefields of ideological and great power hostilities, with discussions, resolutions and voting when it is quite clear that such proceedings cannot produce a valid and effective decision. Although the functions of the Security Council and the General Assembly are in theory distinct, in practice they become confused: they outdo each other in passing resolutions that seem binding but remain ineffective. As a result the authority of the United Nations suffers, while the world forgets that the failures are not the failure of an abstract institution, but of the great powers collectively and individually. People who pay vulgar tribute to Machiavellianism continue to respect the great powers as the real repositories of strength, although they have been seen to be impotent, while the United Nations gets the blame as a hollow, impotent talking-shop — as if there was doubt that the ability of the world organisations to maintain peace is equal to the collective readiness of the members, the great powers, to agree.

Whether the present controversies among the great powers can be reconciled

It may be objected that the faults in the system of great power agreement lie deeper than the lack of proper conventions, that there is a basic absence of a necessary minimum of social, political and ideological agreement. It may be argued that the situation is fundamentally different from what it was under the old European concert of powers, for then there was the more homogeneous society of monarchs and aristocrats, so that when powers voiced their differences, they did so at least in the same language.

But it is important to counter this argument — which is really dogmatic idealism that can only envisage agreement on the basis of shared theories, principles and ideologies. When men launch a common project, be it social, political or whatever, they must of necessity presume the existence of the same reality; and by this yardstick even the most conflicting statements of principle can be evaluated and compensated for in the context of the actual problem. A certain measure of common purpose is necessary, as well as commonly accepted categories and a common language, for it is obvious that if the partners think in very different categories, or mean vastly different things by the same definition, then peace and co-operation will be precarious indeed. But such extreme lack of understanding normally occurs only between people of completely different cultures that have lived entirely isolated from each other — such as the early European explorers and native peoples. And once the two groups have lived and acted together for a time, an identical reality shows up and gives rise to a shared language and outlook : even if it is perhaps limited to the current problems to be faced. On this common ground it is then possible to formulate common interests and action, and to organise peace; though differences will for long survive beneath the common language, occasionally springing traps of misunderstanding and controversy.

But here we draw the line. A lack of understanding resulting from different systems of outlook is one thing. Social, economic, political or ideological conflicts, formulated on a high conceptual level and involving confrontations of interests, or principles, are another. The latter, especially in their first feverish phase, may appear to be irrepressible for reasons of interest or principle; but this is no reason to consider them so. For all their sharpness, such conflicts usually spring from identical categories — for example, between a Christian and a free-thinking atheist who may denounce each other and every tenet the other holds.

Keeping this in mind, we will find that the difficulties impeding great power agreement today are, historically, not unprecedented. The old monarchic-aristocratic Europe could lean on a far more homogeneous social background and system of concepts than is possible today; but though the values of that system should be recognised, we must not idealise it or imagine it to have been free of problems. Before the French Revolution and afterwards, there were monarchies that were more or less controlled by public opinion and monarchies with absolutist systems of government, and the inherent differences impeded agreement between them in matters of foreign policy. Following the revolution of July 1830 the legitimist monarchies increasingly gave way to the advance of constitutionalism, less legitimist monarchies and republics, and from the 1870s onwards there were widely varying political formations: absolute monarchies, more or less constitutional monarchies whose foreign affairs were still directed with absolutist methods, monarchies under the control of public opinion, and parliamentary republics. This could hardly have made great power agreement easier than it is today and, after a fairly long period of peace, it eventually led to the First World War.

The period after the First World War and the fall of European monarchic-feudal legitimacy may contain the most contradictions for the understanding of international politics. The mutual aversion and isolation of the bourgeois democracies and of communism were greater than today, and then there were the hostile feelings between victors and vanquished, between the countries within and outside the world organisation, between those in possession and the dispossessed. Above all there were the fascist countries which subscribed to the principles of domination by the strongest, a racial predestination to dominate, and the invigorating effect of warfare, while they rejected any suggestion of international co-operation and, as a matter of principle, the common ideals of freedom, equal human dignity, democracy on the basis of popular representation and public welfare.

Following the Second World War these confrontations and tensions lost some of their intensity, some even disappeared, and fascism dropped out as a decisive factor. However, in the fluctuations of the cold war, the hostility between bourgeois democracy and communism became of central significance; and further, the political independence of the Third World brought prominence to their confrontation with the white man's international political system. These two areas of confrontation contain the difficulties of the international community today.

In the confrontation between the European and the Third World there is still much mutual incomprehension that plays a major role, transcending economic and social factors. The system in the international community is European in origin, and sprang from the European community of states with its paradoxical tradition of limited warfare. In modern circumstances the institutions and conventions of the international community are both useful and rational. China, for instance, has accepted them, though only partly voluntarily; but whenever she sees fit to turn against the European world, she attacks the institution of diplomatic privilege as one alien to her. Similarly, whenever African peoples are at war with each other, they see the Red Cross as a suspect organisation for helping the enemy – in a concept of a fight to the death, no sympathy can be expected for an institution born of the European concept of limited warfare. However, the aversion of the Third World for European political categories is not today the central factor in the field of international balance. For the future, this may possibly produce sharpened differences in interests and ideals; but at the same time, with increasing world unity, there is the prospect of an increase in mutual misunderstanding.

For great power agreement, the central antagonism today is between bourgeois democracy and communism: on the one hand, hereditary and exploiting private property and free enterprise with the institutions of freedom based on the separation of power; on the other, public ownership of the means of production aimed at the abolition of exploitation, and with a dictatorship, meant to be transitional, and based on the rule of a single party. The antagonism between these is undoubtedly significant and has already cost much blood; and no amount of wishfulness for a synthesis of the two systems will make this antagonism disappear. But at the same time there are influences towards a decrease in the antagonism:

(i) On both sides the fundamental political categories are rooted in the common ideal of freedom. For all their diverging interpretations, both pay tribute to the ultimate ideals of freedom and equal human dignity, to the institutions of democracy based on popular representation and human rights, and to the belief in and search for general welfare for mankind.

(ii) Expressly fascist or crypto-fascist power centres, for all their reappearance in the world, are decidedly in a minority. These oppose such ideals and pay tribute to the omnipotence of violence, to racial supremacy and to the supreme value of life-and-death struggle.

(iii) Both sides contain considerable forces that are trying to lessen the antagonism: on one side this is shown by an effort to contain large-scale private ownership and exploitation; on the other, it is seen in the decrease of certain excesses of the one-party system in the political, economic or cultural fields.

(iv) Among the great powers, the line between the systems is being crossed more and more frequently.

But these factors are counterbalanced, even neutralised, by three political reflexes which produce the present paralysis in great power co-operation:

(i) The ideological slogans of cold war developed by the great powers in the post-war decades aim at reciprocal ideological annihilation. The powers have had to resort to fascist analogies when they have wanted to continue the cold war, to emphasise the irreconcilable nature of their antagonism and the impossibility of serious common conventions. They have tried to show the symptoms of Hitlerite paranoia in their opponents so as to be able to classify them as fascist, and for this purpose the West applies the expression 'totalitarianism' to communism, and the communist countries apply the expressions 'monopolistic capitalism' and 'imperialism' to the Western world. This kind of warfare is not only deceptive but also suicidal. It is vital for mankind that these categories should not become hollow slogans used in bad faith, and that a political paranoia of truly Nazi proportions should not reappear.

(ii) Realpolitik is used to try to acquire and defend power, strategic and economic positions, without regard for ideals or principles – by turning supposedly irreconcilable ideals into politics. This will lead to the use of violence which will tragically undermine ideological positions, and thus bring a political amorality, dangerous for the protagonists and for others. In this atmosphere, any concession or show of good faith to the opponent will be seen as political naivete and betrayal of the cause. This will shake faith in the principles of great power policies and produce political nihilism, and it will seriously impede the evolution and stability of conventions for international coexistence.

(iii) All this will then lead to the deterioration of the techniques of international intercourse and negotiation, that is, the inability to negotiate.

This does not mean that existing differences of interest, ideology and power considerations can or should be abolished so that the hidden possibilities of great power agreement can be discovered and its institutions function. What it means is that the differences should be raised to a higher level, and that this is the only way to validate the tenet explained earlier: that the great powers must pursue policies that are superior in level and degree of responsibility to the policies of other countries, for only then can the institutions of great power agreement function. What is needed are policies that contain and comprehend self-interest on a wider and higher level, rather than naive and self-denying policies. The great powers ought to think in terms of a global and complex balance of ideas, ideologies and positions, and should realise that in the twentieth century there is no sense in envisaging the confrontation of powers or ideas, or insisting on power zones and spheres of influence, Monroe or other doctrines, opposing camps. They must be aware that, given the present state of economics, power, ideas and public consciousness, power-military-economic positions and conceptual-moral-ideological positions are interchangeable in the same way as matter and energy are interchangeable in the understanding of modern physics.

In practice this means that if political wisdom or considerations of principle and morals are allowed to influence power positions at one point of the globe, this may produce a moral capital that may bring interest in terms of increased power positions somewhere else and at some other time; and similarly, if a position is maintained by means of maximum coercion, this may result in a loss of moral capital that may lead to serious loss of power positions elsewhere.

Ideological confrontation is not simply a confrontation of good and evil: every so-called ideological system is a mixture of right and topical programmes with wrong and outmoded ones. So in the field of ideologies victory is scored when the right and topical elements win over the wrong and outmoded ones within the limits of one's own ideology, and not by one ideology opposing another one. Therefore the world powers should not bargain over the national and conceptual values in their trust, but, conceiving these on a higher plane, they should get out of their deadlocked attitudes, and then the law of common reality would make it possible, indeed force them, to create a limited common system of categories and idiom. Then common interests could be recognised and common actions planned, thus solving concrete disputes and averting the worst disasters. And gradually agreements might evolve that in their totality could be tantamount to world peace.

In this regard, China's present political system and the rest of the world contain a relationship that is a new phenomenon and a disquieting one. There is a good measure of mutual incomprehension based on the differences between fundamental categories, and there is a sharp antagonism of interests and ideals. To the rest of the world, China represents the traditions and system of categories of a highly developed culture that is vastly different from the European. It is a culture that is earlier in origin than Europe's and, though its force has been somewhat blunted in recent centuries, it has been aimed at rationalising, humanising and giving moral strength to politics and power. China also forcefully shows all the turmoil and revulsion of the Third World caused by European colonialism and the white world. And she has exclusive claim to the initial, most intransigent phase of communist revolution, that is fraught with the very dangerous ideology of glorifying the life-and-death struggle in the 'wars of liberation'. For the time being we must fear in this a strong negative attitude towards the functioning of great power agreement.

The new role of the United Nations' Secretary General and the function of international mediation

We have implied that the institutionalisation of international co-operation in the United Nations and other specialist organisations has not brought any important advance to the basic problems of war and peace. Indeed it has made it possible for the direct responsibility of the great powers to become obscured.

However, this institutionalisation can boast improved possibilities for international co-operation in the evolution of the United Nations Secretariat and the Secretary General. The Charter of the United Nations gives wider scope for initiative and mediation by the Secretary General, over a broad range of international problems, than did the Covenant of the League of Nations; and successive Secretaries General have taken the initiative in a variety of contexts.

In evaluating the function of the Secretary General and the Secretariat, we must go back to our premise that what is now needed is not a world government, but simply the better functioning of the agencies of great power agreement, together with the emergence of institutions of impartial arbitration on the basis of known principles. It would be a gross mistake to see an embryonic world government in the administrative organisation of the Secretariat, or to force it in that direction, however similar to a collection of global ministries it may be. The Secretary General, as the executive officer of the Security Council, is by definition of his function an impartial agent. He may have an important part to play in improving the operation of great power agreement and in helping the institutions of impartial arbitration and their decisions on matters of principle. Within the limits of classical international concepts, the essence of his function may be seen in the institutionalisation of the previously informal and occasional acts of 'good offices' and mediation. In other words, he is a modern and institutionalised mediator and peace-maker. The prevalent democratically based societies prescribe a more diverse international organisation than at present exists; within this the mediator could link the Security Council with proposed agencies and procedures of impartial arbitration in matters of principle; thus power and favourable balance would be secured by the one, and decisions which can command loyalty and legitimacy in the public mind by the other. Today only the first role — promotion of great power agreement — is to the fore. The Secretaries

General have often had eminent success in this, although admittedly only in matters not directly linked with the central issues that divide the great powers.

Successive Secretaries have developed rather differing practices in the interpretation of their eminently political role. Immediately preceding the tragic death of the second Secretary General, Count Bernadotte, there was a full-scale international crisis during which he was accused of pursuing his own policies and of not being sufficiently impartial. The next Secretary General was rightly aware that, no matter how political his function, he could not afford to evolve his own personal policy in the sense that a great power or statesman can. But he may have slightly exaggerated the situation when, in pleading mortal danger for world peace, he almost made a programme out of the freezing of provisional situations in the search for final settlement. If it would be dangerous to pursue the search for 'solutions at any price' that used to characterise the fascist regimes, the search for final settlements in the interests of peace and stability, and a registration of the means, should be associated with the function of universal mediator – as evolved for the Secretary General.

Comprehensive international political transactions for peace and stability

An international mediator and peacemaker who was able to link the agencies of great power agreement with those of impartial arbitration could be much more comprehensive in the approach to problems imperilling world peace and stability. On such a basis it would be possible to negotiate far more comprehensive political solutions.

As we have seen, the political transactions of the old monarchic Europe based on mutual concessions and compensations, services and counter-services, became rather outmoded when the principle of self-determination became prevalent. William III, King of England, was a master of the old system when he tried unsuccessfully to avert the War of the Spanish Succession with a multitude of plans for partition and succession. Other masters of the system were Charles VI and Cardinal Fleury, authors of the European settlements between the Wars of the Spanish and Austrian successions; and then there were the politicians who took part in the Congress of Vienna. It is also worth noticing the 1735 Vienna Peace Treaty that concluded the war for the Polish throne. It solved all the outstanding problems of Europe in one coherent transaction, like a chain reaction: it found the solution for the war for the Polish throne, for the compensation of the unsuccessful Polish pretender, for France's efforts to annex Lorraine, for the compensation of the ducal House of Lorraine, for the problem of the expected extinction of the grand ducal House of Tuscany, and for the Austro-Spanish rivalry over possessions in Italy.

Since the predominance of democratic social principles, these transactions have been condemned as ruthless exchanges of subjects. But, in a different way, without severely offending democratic principles – indeed even in their service – such ararangements would make sense today. In many aspects the world needs solutions to conflicts in the form of a package deal of mutual concessions and conditions, or a chain of territorial and other concessions, in order to lift matters out of the deadlock brought about by the inflexibility of the parties. It may be worth illustrating this with a few examples, and to begin with an opportunity missed – in the Portuguese colonies in India.

All sober observers could see that the official Portuguese argument that the inhabitants of Goa would be integrated with the Portuguese nation was unrealistic. The Portuguese claimed that the Goans enjoyed a better administration and a higher standard of living than their neighbours; but racially and linguistically they were identical with the neighbouring Indian population, and few of them were Christians. Given the relative forces of India and Portugal, it was clear that it was only a matter of time before the Indians would overcome scruples about applying coercion; and the fact that she was prepared to wait for a fairly long time shows that she would seriously have appreciated a chance to settle the matter peacefully. The great powers, particularly the Western ones, should have been able to press Portugal to concede her Indian colonies to India before it was too late, or to let their fate be decided by an impartial forum; and India in exchange should have been willing to submit the Kashmir question to either arbitration, adjudication or perhaps plebiscite. But such an arrangement was steadfastly opposed by India for over twenty years. Such a peaceful arrangement would have contributed precisely the motive needed for the solution of the Kashmir problem through an impartial procedure. The Western powers would have had ample means to combine pressure on Portugal with some compensation, but they were not inclined to become involved in transactions so far outside their immediate concern. Today, after one of the issues has been settled by force, and the other, after a bloody conflict, is as unsettled as ever, they have reason to regret having missed this and other opportunities to help the cause of world peace and stability, and at the same time to add to their non-moral and political capital.

Gibraltar provides another example where a possible transaction could be conceived in the interests of peace, stability and justice. This is still a live situation, but without a clear formulation of the basic questions. The position of national adherence by the population of Gibraltar is confused by the repellent character of the present Spanish regime and by the materialistic consideration of Gibraltar's higher standard of living. In this situation a referendum would be a mere political manoeuvre and not a true application of the principle of self-determination. But if a British government saw it as politically expedient to return Gibraltar to a freer

Spain, this could be tied up with another territorial condition that would be justified for peace and stability: namely the return of Ceuta by Spain to Morocco – which provides the same thorn in Morocco's flesh as Gibraltar does in Spain's – regardless of the fact that its inhabitants, like those of Gibraltar, probably enjoy a higher standard of living and administration than their brothers in Morocco. Such a political transaction might also become desirable for preventing future conflicts.

It is largely up to the great powers to launch such transactions, which could often be done within the context of the abolition of their own remaining colonies. After all, they possess great resources of power and ideals, and they are not reduced to insisting on pettily conceived territorial integrity. At the same time it may be suggested that these and similar possibilities might well become part of functions of the Secretary General as a mediator, so that he may, at the suitable moment, submit the suggestion to the interested parties. But this could only happen with the involvement of impartial procedures and agencies as yet uncreated.

The contractual nature of great power agreements

Let us consider the probable results if a development of practical conventions of co-operation within the world organisation should come into being, and so provide the conditions for international agreement and great power agreement in particular, and thus allow the Security Council to function more consistently and efficiently. (Agreement, of course, depends upon an easing of tensions between the great power groupings.) And let us assume in this case that the function of the Secretary General as mediator betweeen the great powers will be broader and more successful.

In effect there will be better and more durable international treaties. While the function of the Security Council may be to pass binding resolutions, these will remain in essence treaties containing political compromise. Although there are important elements of impartial arbitration by a superior authority in the decisions taken by the Security Council – the decisions in its provisional function over state-formations and territorial status in the trusteeship territories moving towards independence – these are still mostly compromises motivated by political and practical considerations, and not by principles. Similarly, the Security Council resolutions over the admission of new United Nations members are compromises rather than impartial decisions. In its way the older procedure of diplomatic recognition was the admission of members to the international community, and the new procedure, owing its nature to compromise, is not much more advanced than the old – and, besides, several examples show that it gives no guarantee against the creation of new states that have no serious chance of nation-formation, or ability to maintain real independence. In other words, even if the Security Council has great success, its function will remain the conclusion of international treaties based on compromise, and we cannot reasonably expect anything else.

We have seen how the prevalence of democratic social principles, especially the principle of self-determination, has considerably weakened the effectiveness of international treaties in giving state-formations and territorial changes legitimacy in the public mind and in stimulating loyalty to the changes. Since the common will of kings has ceased to be an undisputed source of legitimacy, it is only possible for great power agreement or international treaties to achieve stable results when they are able to restore, confirm or justify already existing and undisputed legitimacies; and it is only in rare and fortunate instances that they can create an international will that reflects the basic principle of the international community and is a suitable source of legitimacy. Hence, even if the institutional functioning of great power agreement is greatly improved, and there is the more variegated international organisation that is prescribed by the principle of self-determination, fundamental questions of principle still require an impartial international procedure – plebiscite – and impartial arbitration as exceptional forums.

The main function of great power agreement will continue to be the prevention and elimination of war, and the provision of an international police for operating the impartial organisation; and the latter will only function in critical situations in order to apply the fundamental governing principles rooted in common conviction in the settling of important problems of principle such as state-formation and territorial changes. The international organisation thus channels the functioning of power forces more towards principles, and ensures that new situations quickly become stable, comprehensive and legitimate, with peoples loyal to them. In practice such an organisation can only be an impartial international political tribunal.

[11]

Towards International Political Arbitration

The first efforts to secure a system of international political arbitration

The International Court of Justice and the various international specialist courts are regarded as impartial forums by international law today. But in intention and practice they are concerned with questions relating to the content and application of ordinary international law, and not with the ultimate principles of the international community in disputes over state-formation or territorial settlements. Yet the European peace movements at the turn of the century pinned great hopes on the creation of such courts as impartial bodies, and they expected them to eliminate war and to settle political conflicts peacefully. What caused these expectations and why were they disappointed? And if an impartial forum could fulfil these expectations, then what kind of a forum if not the ordinary international court?

There are historical precedents in international political arbitration when protagonists have chosen a disinterested party to arbitrate between them. In Europe since the Middle Ages there have been several precedents when the Pope or another chosen arbiter was required to decide between contestants. But this could never provide a permanent institution, and in more modern times arbitration was allowed to decline for under royal absolution the personal will of the sovereign was the central factor in domestic and international action. Differences could be settled by the physical clash of wills – opposing but not trying to annihilate each other – and subsequent compromise. Under the modern monarchies mediators were often invited to arbitrate; and great power conventions used every means of political craft to hammer out compromises rather than reach decisions based on principles. From the time of the Congress of Vienna monarchic Europe was on the defensive – at Vienna the concert of powers nearly established impartial procedures through the fairly consistent application of principles formulated on the basis of legitimacy by Talleyrand. But there was no need then for impartial agencies or procedures with distinct functions beyond the political activities of the great powers in conference and of broader international conferences, which more or less assumed the role of arbitrators.

Impartial political arbitration was a function of the change from monarchic-feudal legitimacy to the principle of self-determination, and this was its importance for the international community. So from the mid-nineteenth century the need for modern forms of international arbitration has shown itself, and it has reflected the disturbed balance that was part of the slow transition from one basic principle to the other as the European community gradually merged into a global international community.

The international peace movements were the first to demand that conflicts between states be settled through peaceful arbitration; but with this idealism went recognition that democratic social principles tolerate far less arbitration than the aristocratic principles, and yet demand fuller effect: hence the prescription for some impartial agency and procedure. Two facts underlined this need: first, the renewal of wars in the mid-nineteenth century showed how frightful warfare had become through technical progress and compulsory military service; secondly, the contradiction between the monarchic framework which was still almost intact in Europe, and the new tensions between national movements that gradually replaced the antagonisms between sovereigns, made these wars increasingly meaningless.

This demand for impartial political arbitration could not succeed, given the characteristics of the international community of the time. Though it corresponded to a real need, it was premature because: (a) the European concert with its monarchic tradition still functioned, and it was still capable of overcoming the problem of a war between two adversaries, so the states did not feel the necessity of submitting their basic political, territorial power disputes to arbitration; (b) the monarchies could not afford to embrace the principle of self-determination without exposing themselves to mortal danger, while the national movements could not accept the monarchic principle which for them was hopelessly outdated, so the very basis of principle upon which such disputes might have been settled through arbitration was also a disputed subject. In fact throughout the nineteenth century no impartial arbitrator was allowed to touch a grave political conflict.

The influence of the efforts to secure a political arbitration on the development of regular international arbitration

At the same time it became clear that there was need for regular international arbitration. An extensive system of international law had evolved over the course of centuries, and in the nineteenth century the sudden expansion of international commercial and other contracts created increased numbers of minor disputes requiring settlement. These were not the basic questions of state-formation or boundaries that were important enough for states to fight over, and so they had no decisive influence on the need to settle political conflicts peacefully. Such peaceful settlement at most lessened minor frictions between individual countries. But from the mid-nineteenth century onwards the situation evolved whereby states would submit to elected arbitrators their secondary, purely legal disputes which contained no dangers of war; and did so with ovations from the international peace movements.

Expectations of the success of such international arbitration were nourished by the first major case in which an elected tribunal settled an international legal dispute. This involved the British-built ship 'Alabama' which was used as a confederate commerce raider during the Civil War in the United States. It set a precedent for countries to settle a legal dispute peacefully when tension existed between the two; but it was to become the source of illusions that would last for decades, particularly since the losing party honoured the tribunal's decision. It became rooted in the public mind that the threat of Anglo-American war had been averted by submission of the issue to arbitration, when, as a matter of fact, this took place only after the Civil War had ended and when, despite bellicose propaganda, it was unlikely that either party would want to fight over this dispute. Here the alternative to arbitration was not so much open war as a series of mutual retributions. And the case was not one of state-formation or territorial adjustment involving basic governing principles. The tribunal only had to decide, in ordinary international law, on the duties of a neutral country at a time of civil strife in another country, and what compensation should be paid for any unlawful damages caused.

Similarly the Hague Peace Conferences hardly justified the hopes they occasioned. At the time the growing intensity of the armaments race had made it vital that there should be arbitration capable of averting war, although arbitration in fact failed to materialise for the reasons already discussed. Indeed some countries, notably Germany, opposed even the purely legal type of international arbitration. The only achievements of the Hague Conferences were to clarify some disputed questions concerning the laws of war, and the creation of the Permanent Court of Arbitration — which was hardly more than a register of elected judges with a secretariat. This could also have performed the functions of an international political tribunal, but the judges on the register were all prominent practitioners of codified international law, and countries continued to refuse to bring their disputes concerning states-formation or territorial issues to the Permanent Court of Arbitration or to any other court.

After the First World War, those who had hoped for peace in the world felt that international arbitration had been unable to prevent the outbreak of war, and they turned their backs on it; and even international peace movements showed far less enthusiasm over the Permanent

International Court of Justice established within the framework of the League of Nations. After the Second World War the International Court of Justice of the United Nations was to replace this as the permanent court competent to decide legal disputes on the basis of international law. But the binding nature of the verdicts of both these courts was never accepted by all the states, and even those that did excluded the so-called vital, political issues – which covered virtually all the problems arising from state-formation, and all the territorial and political issues which had been largely responsible for wars. And the international courts themselves would consistently evade the responsibility whenever such cases were presented to them, claiming that they could not pass judgement on such matters. They assumed, almost always correctly, that there was no way of securing the effectiveness of such a judgement.

So, in the history of efforts to bring about modern international arbitration and jurisdiction the call for international arbitration has always been voiced either to avert war or to settle conflicts arising out of war or civil war, while the agencies of arbitration and jurisdiction have repeatedly tended to follow the well-trodden path of ordinary international jurisdiction, confined to strictly legal decisions. In this way the various peace movements have succeeded in bringing about the creation of an ordinary international jurisdiction whose function is the extension of the rule of law to important new fields, but which has no part whatever in the prevention of war. As a result, in the twentieth century regular international arbitration for the purpose of interpreting law has been well established, but the problem of exceptional international political arbitration, concerned with questions of state-formation as well as political and territorial issues, has remained a separate and open question.

The difference between international political arbitration and regular international arbitration

A distinction should be recognised between political arbitration, which is concerned with issues of state-formation, political and territorial questions, and regular arbitration in issues of international law. The difference is that a court of arbitration consists of judges or arbitrators elected by the contestants, while a court of law consists of permanent judges; the difference is not that between judgements over political and over legal matters since, in principle, submissions concerning both of these may be made to either court. While existing international courts resort to international law, the Statute of the International Court of Justice expressly allows the courts to arrive at decisions on the basis of equity if this is what the contestants require – so in principle it would be quite possible to put political cases before the International Court of Justice, although this has never been done and it is not likely to be done in the future.

The two kinds of arbitration contain a decisive difference in their function. Under the present circumstances, political arbitration must needs be an exceptional procedure for applying the basic principles of the constitution of the international community; its authority to pronounce general and binding verdicts will not be accepted in the foreseeable future. So there must be no confusing of this with regular international jurisdiction, which, on account of the explosive expansion of international relations, is expected to extend the rule of law over a wide field. This should best develop in the direction of compulsory arbitration, maybe in legal matters of international effect, in the direction of international high court jurisdiction. But international political arbitration must preserve more of its character as voluntarily accepted arbitration by a tribunal elected by the litigants.

Another fundamental difference is in the relationships between the judges and the procedures and rules, and hence in the attitudes of the arbitrators. For political arbitration, especially in its initial state, there are no readily available rules outside the basic principle and the practical problem; the rules must be formulated by the agency for arbitration. But for ordinary international arbitration there is an extensive system of rules and precedents available, even if it is a freer system than domestic jurisdiction within individual states. If an international court of justice is presented with a case that cannot be accommodated by the system of rules and precedents, the court is very much inclined to plead lack of competence and to refuse it. But this is what must not happen when it comes to political arbitration, with its fewer rules but wider field of competence.

For understanding the essential function of such arbitration, domestic jurisdiction with its longer and more varied evolution provides useful analogies. At first sight it might seem that it does not have the same flexibility, because of its more complex and developed character – but flexibility is basic to jurisdiction even in the domestic law of individual states. At the beginning there were no complex procedures or concrete rules, but only the dispute itself with one or more quite general principles concerning it – principles variously interpreted or in apparent contradiction – and the awareness that a decision must be reached or the dispute would be aggravated. The arbitrator must decide even in the absence of established rules. This is the core of the theory that the judge precedes the law, and procedural rules take precedence over rules relating to the merits of the case; but if the existing rules are too rigid or insufficient there is need for a freer application of the law on more sophisticated levels. This was shown in the special jurisdiction of the 'people's right' (*ius gentium*) of Roman civil law, and in the principle of 'equity' in British common law. Both of these needed a long process of evolution, and both were increasingly to affect regular jurisdiction until they became an integral part of its system of agencies, procedures and rules.

No trend exists towards the merging of international political arbitration with regular jurisdiction in the foreseeable future; so with this in mind we must look at another analogy from domestic law: constitutional jurisdiction. The function of this is to apply the articles of the constitution: the fundamental law of the state. The complex and highly developed constitutional jurisdiction of individual states is based on more than principles, it also has its codified constitutional law, but in its functioning the ultimate basic principles — sovereignty of the people, human rights, representation, social and economic structure, etc. — are of decisive importance. Though this is as yet very distant, the best hope for international political arbitration would be to become an international constitutional jurisdiction.

The necessity for and absence of international political arbitration since the end of the First World War

At the end of the First World War there was general acceptance of the principle of self-determination as the common basic governing principle: the first and fundamental precondition of political arbitration as distinct from regular international jurisdiction. As we know, there was still no real political arbitration in the course of the post-war settlements; and since, in spite of high hopes, European public opinion expected such arbitration from supra-national organisations especially because international courts had been unable to avert war. The traumatic experiences of the war militated against there being any impartial procedure that could have benefited the losers as well as the victors. The victors thought they would safeguard their own interests better if they did not give impartial bodies the right to make decisions; and besides, they felt quite able to make the ultimate decisions in matters of state-formation and territorial disputes, just as the kings had done before them when applying the monarchic principle to dynastic disputes.

So the experts were only consulted in a rather minor capacity or limited terms of reference for questions where the Allies or the League of Nations considered it necessary to ask their opinion; and they were consulted whenever bargains or insurrections necessitated a referendum, and the conduct of the referendum produced associated questions. Only one of these decisions reached the level and authority of true political arbitration, and this only because of the expertise and impartiality of its author and not on account of its procedural authority. This was Lord Curzon's decision over the Polish-Soviet frontier. In the circumstances this could not attain validity, but it was still a live force a quarter of a century later when the present Polish-Soviet frontier was drawn up.

The situation after the Second World War was essentially the same as after the First, though aggravated by the fact that even faith in the principle of self-determination was no longer intact. In the course of the peace negotiations the French government raised the possibility of political arbitration over disputed political matters, but without any particular reaction on the part of others.

During the following years experts were consulted over widely varying matters to do with self-determination or referenda which were occasioned by the liberation of trusteeship territories by the United Nations or of colonies through wars or bargaining. On these occasions the experts were asked to take a stand tantamount to giving a decision but, once again, no fully fledged and independent arbitration took place over any significant issue.

No procedure of real value on the basis of self-determination has ever been applied in practice, and the use of experts, whilst still ocasionally employed, has been futile and brought no results. However great their expertise and impartiality, the experts, referendum committees, delegated commissions, etc., in their subordinate positions and within their narrow terms of reference have had no real personal responsibility as arbitrators and have not formed integral parts of a united institution. So it has been impossible for them to evolve a uniform routine, and often they have even contributed to the confusion of concepts themselves through applying a blend of important considerations of principle with pure expediency (such as has been mentioned concerning the Mosul dispute). So they have often sanctioned solutions which, far from promoting self-determination and nation-formation, have actually impeded or annulled them.

At the same time there was desperate need for impartial procedures and agencies to take the place of the extinct system of treaties of the old monarchies, with their suggested legitimacy and their command of loyalty. The reasons that induced some countries and great powers not to employ such agencies and procedures have since proved insufficient and futile: it transpired that the peacemaking ability of the supra-national organisations was not even as great as that of the old monarchies; circumvention of impartial procedures, far from canalising the fear of war, rendered it permanent; only very narrow and short-term interests could be served when a *fait accompli* or right of decision was successfully set against principles, and in the long run this brought damage and dangers for all; and it turned out that the great powers had little control over the application of the principle of self-determination, while their actual activity has consisted of sanctioning given situations and mediation of negligible value gained through painful bargaining and compromise.

The difficulties and possibilities of international political arbitration

We may doubt if there is any point in discussing political arbitration, since individual states are reluctant to accept normal international jurisdiction in purely legal matters and have never once submitted to political arbitration over vital matters containing threat of war, though offered to them again and again; and the more so since there is little of the old enthusiasm for the establishment of impartial agencies, or public recognition of the need for them. But if we observe that the occasions for political arbitration have occurred only in the past fifty years, since general acceptance of the basic principle of self-determination, we will realise that the most decisive chances of applying it properly have been missed.

There appear to be three main arguments against the prospect of political arbitration becoming seriously institutionalised: (i) the condition of impartiality does not prevail — there are no persons or agencies unaffected by opposing interests in a world where different, even contrary political, social, economic and moral systems confront each other; (ii) insurmountable intransigence is shown by countries, in times of peace, in defence of their territorial integrity, their possessions, political and economic interests, in the face of any claims or suggestion that these claims be put before an impartial forum; (iii) even if the parties concerned are willing to make such a concession, the great powers who wield the political options of intervention, mediation or decision, are opposed to any transfer of their options to impartial agencies and procedures.

The first argument, that impartiality is impossible, is characteristic of disillusioned idealism. It is an attitude that involves formulating unrealistic requirements and, when they are shown to be unfeasible, refuting even what is feasible with dogmatic generalisations, thus supporting the theoretical and practical exponents of unlimited coercion. This argument is exactly the same in form as the claim that the antagonism between the great powers is irreconcilable. But in fact what is necessary for international arbitration and for great power agreement is not absolute impartiality — it is even doubtful if this expression has any meaning at all — but only impartiality relating to a certain given situation. Such impartiality can be found and used whenever it has a function. Peaceful coexistence is only possible because it is also possible to find a few men able to satisfy the maximum requirements of impartiality to carry out the function of impartial arbitration and to exert corresponding psychological influence — although not with the philosophical certainty of absolute impartiality.

As for the second argument, the resistance of the countries concerned, in every dispute there are, of course, those who are in possession and those who are not, and those who are in full possession are usually difficult to persuade into making concessions or accepting impartial arbitration — which is equivalent to making a concession. This is particularly true when the dispute concerns territorial status. But as we have shown, the more secure a state feels itself, the less it is governed by force, and the more it represents higher values and causes rather than physical existence and power, and the more it is inclined to tolerate the right to self-determination even when that involves a claim on part of its own territory. There have been many examples of this, and we may hope that there will be many more. We have also shown that, while it is difficult to envisage general acceptance of a forum of arbitration with the authority to reach binding decisions concerning questions of state-formation, territorial or political disputes, it is possible to envisage even the less politically mature countries allowing an exceptional procedure – political arbitration – to be used when this is imperative because of the complex or threatening nature of the situation, and when it is encouraged by a certain state of balance, the weight of great powers, the possibility of compensation, or other international factors.

The third argument against the feasibility of international political arbitration is the weightiest: the resistance of the great powers and, through them, of the agencies of great power agreement to transferring the authority to arbitrate to an impartial body, even when the parties directly concerned are willing to allow it. A habit of thought leads people to believe it politically wise to hold exclusive power – and hence to think it good policy to seek out the minor, petty, perhaps commercial considerations in order to bring the case within a country's power interests through a claim to direct interest. Because of this a power may easily make concessions in vital matters so long as this can be done within its customary framework of bargaining, rather than accept an expert and impartial agency working on the basis of principles. If a power is forced by circumstances to employ such an agency it is inclined to treat it and its procedures as an alien body in the system of politics, as an imponderable factor, and will try to confine it to the subordinate role of expert advisor.

The harmful nature of this safeguarding of interests which fails to achieve its purpose has been amply shown by events. In fact the real interest of most countries including the great powers is for the greatest possible increase in world stability, and it is not primarily to see that their individual affairs are settled advantageously, nor is it for them to secure the maximum right to interfere in the affairs of others in pursuit of their own interests, much less than existing disputes should continue and grow worse. This is particularly true today when mankind's physical existence is threatened. The true self-interest of individual countries and of the international community appears on the surface selfless from the angle of primitive Machiavellism: it can only be served by that blending of social and psychological factors which must be created by decisions based on long-term principles; only thus can fluid, unsettled, provisional positions, legacies of the past, and future problems, be resolved into situations which can claim undisputed legitimacy through the strength and authority of the agencies and procedures behind them. This is how to secure the support of public agreement and the loyalty of the countries and populations concerned.

But as we know from experience, these simple truths are seldom learnt through rational thought — more often it is through crises, shocks, catastrophes, damages difficult to repair. If, either in spite of or on account of this, we still dare believe that the evolution of the agencies and procedures of impartial international political arbitration will provide a utopia less ambitious and more realistic than a world government, then the following arguments may bring hope in the face of the counter-arguments, particularly that of great power intransigence:

(i) There is a cumulative effect in the alarming experiences, the harm and the danger that are inherent in the situations brought about by compromise and interim solutions conceived to safeguard short-term interests. This is not only a moral damage, but an appalling cost in human lives (largely borne by the small nations involved in petty differences); and a cost in terms of material values (partly borne by the great powers in defence of their interests), spreading a fear of the future on small and great. These considerations may all contribute to a more farsighted great power policy, the need for which has already been mentioned in discussing regeneration of the agencies of great power agreement.

(ii) The inability of states, including great powers, to negotiate has the effect of increasingly obstructing bargains, even purely political ones. Though great power agreement is a more primary condition of international co-operation, a blockage of negotiations may still produce curious situations in which impartial arbitration may appear an alternative to deadlocked talks, providing a way out which secures interests and prestige.

(iii) The characteristic political concepts of bargain, compensation, mutual concession and balance may be integral parts of political arbitration and the application of democratic principles.

(iv) Once agreement to it is reached, impartial international arbitration will hardly raise the thorny problems of execution and organisation — unlike the more ambitious goal of world government — provided that the first experiments justify the procedure, and that it may begin the critical initial phase of institutionalisation.

On the basis of this, all that we will say about the possible features, organisation, terms of reference, binding nature and contents of impartial international political arbitration is subject to the hope and assumption that it will become a reality in the future.

Basic features and possible organisation of international political arbitration

Now we can clearly formulate the chief requirements for such international political arbitration.

1. The terms of reference of the agency must be exceptional, not general and binding. In operating it will follow the initiative of either the interested parties or of international bodies, and it will operate in a favourable state of balance, to settle disputes or critical issues.

2. For all its exceptional nature, it must also be institutional, so that even though its operation is not continuous it may establish an uninterrupted routine. An agency must have some such identity in order to become an integral part of the development of international law, and so that it can acquire the necessary authority, and gradually evolve the procedural forms and rules which may serve as catalysts of common conviction for giving concrete form to the international legal community's basic principles.

3. It must be impartial and independent so that its decisions appear as the valid application of the generally accepted ultimate principles. Only this way can the decisions have the necessary authority and legitimising force, and command loyalty, such as will replace international agreements which are no longer fully capable of performing this function.

4. Despite its impartiality and independence, it must be political in the sense that its decisions are motivated by political judgement rather than through applying the rules of law or just clarifying facts. Its function is to give concrete form to the basic principles of the international community on questions of demarcation in the international legal community, which has hitherto been unformulated in legal terms. In so doing it must weigh what is possible politically with what is correct conceptually in order to see what steps may be taken at any time towards solving an objective problem on the basis of principles. So it has to find solutions that will be able to withstand foreseeable pressures and simultaneously represent the application and continuous development of principles.

It is premature to discuss in any detail the organisational forms which would follow from these basic features. However, the agency's institutional nature which is necessary to secure continuity and authority requires more than a simple secretariat and list of judges, such as constituted the Permanent Court of International Justice created in 1899. There is no need for the agency to operate frequently, or to consist of professional and permanent members, but it must have some corporate organisational form so that it may be able to produce a coherent view or opinion as occasion arises. There would probably be a phase when the method would become 'fashionable' through occasional arbitrations; and the Secretary General of the United Nations may have an important part to play in bringing these about. A permanent agency can be created only after the authority of the method has been established and it may consist of arbitrators who have already worked on an *ad hoc* basis. It will obviously be useful to give the contending parties the option to choose the arbitrators either from a list provided or without reference to it. But even so, in order to strengthen the guarantees of a corporate decision and of impartiality, the permanent agency ought to play an increasing role in appointing or delegating chairmen, in providing lists or appointing or delegating additional arbitrators to already existing tribunals. The composition of the permanent agency should be increasingly through co-option, giving the international political agencies, such as the Security Council or the General Assembly, the right of veto rather than the right of appointment.

Equally important is the question: from whom should the arbitrators be drawn? For this, moral and intellectual qualities are obviously more relevant than expertise. As for professional aptness, rather than setting positive qualifications there are two sets of people who should be excluded: jurists specialised in strictly codified international law, and active politicians deeply involved in international or domestic power politics. Anyone between these two extremes may be considered: international officials with experience in mediation and conciliation, scholars of law or politics, political essayists or journalists, national and international politicians not in the focus of power politics and known to be conciliatory in their attitudes, especially politicians of traditionally neutral countries, etc., or the kind of people who have had experience as United Nations mediators appointed by the Secretary General.

Possible terms of reference, and decisions of an international political tribunal

First and foremost among the terms of reference of such an agency is, obviously enough, decision-making over all territorial disputes which lend themselves to arbitration as the alternative to settlement by power relations or violence – this occurring either through the will of the participants or through the intervention of great powers or international organs. Such disputes have raised the need for an agency in the first place; and in them the stakes are usually high enough to justify the creation of a new agency within the framework of the international community.

Once such an agency has been created it may also be used for some other purposes; for example, where there are proposals or movements towards the formation of new states, the agency could weigh up whether a projected state contains the elements of realistic nation-formation, or whether it could be a focal point for the gradual formation of a new nation, and whether it could aspire to membership of the international community – the United Nations.

Another purpose for the agency could arise when there is the possibility of suspending a state's membership of the international organisations, or suspending rights due under international law. This could happen when a state fails to allow even a minimum of legal human rights, or the most elemetary requirements of political morality as set by the rest of the community. While it would be dangerous and impossible to prescribe governmental and social systems for the members of the international community, the lessons of the twentieth century have shown that, allowing for suitable guarantees, it should be possible for such sanctions to be taken against a country that, for example, adopted a system of slavery, political gangsterism or paranoid dictatorship, or sought power on the basis of racism or another irrational ideology. In such a case if one international political bloc were to organise sanctions against the offending state it would almost invite the opposing political bloc to defend the delinquent; and sanctions may easily lose credibility if they become a political weapon. The agencies of the United Nations could suspend or limit membership rights of a state with more weight, but the weight would be far greater if the sanctioning was undertaken by an impartial agency of arbitration.

In the context of these additional functions, it would be up to the organisation of international political arbitration to define 'minimum political and legal morality'. Less than this minimum would be cause for refusal of membership of the international community and could lead to the denying of development and other international aid to offenders.

Such a minimum should require more than stability of administrative power — the traditional international prerequisite of recognition — as this can occasionally be attained by slave-owning, racist and other terrorist regimes. But it must not be concerned with the differences between social and political systems, for the minimum requirements must reflect the common basic principles of the entire international community. And this minimum requirement should not coincide with the high-level institutions of formal democracy and rule of law (nation-wide representation, securing of the rule of law in full depth, etc.), for if this were to be demanded of a country regardless of its political and cultural maturity, it would inevitably lead to the creation of pseudo-institutions functioning with false methods — especially in developing countries.

What should be prescribed is a minimum basis for the further development of administration, politics and law — including local and corporate self-government, specialisation of administrative and juridical functions, elementary human rights, civil equality, minority rights, basic freedom of movement, protection against exploitation, allowance for criticism, etc. These political conditions of recognition, membership or aid would be independent of the differences among the world systems and would be supported by the authority of the entire international community, and they would justify fewer objections than today's conditions – which are chiefly concerned with the attitude of the new state to the opposing systems and blocs and sometime flagrantly ignore the shortcomings of public life within the country concerned.

So far as the obligatory nature of the arbitration is concerned, it is important that the tribunal should be authorised to pass binding resolutions, but it is also essential that it should be able to express opinions, and sanction existing situations, on the basis of principles.

The agency should be able to express opinions, especially in the early stages when great powers and political world organisations would find it difficult to relinquish the power of making decisions, and contending parties would be even more reluctant to give *carte blanche* to the arbitrators. An opinion might possibly be given without the consent of the parties concerned in response to requests by international bodies, in particular the Security Council. Of course this would only make sense if such an opinion gave legitimacy and a programme of action to a functioning great power agreement; otherwise, like the regular international courts of justice, the arbitrators would probably refrain from expressing opinions which would in all likelihood be rejected. In order to overcome the mistrust of contending parties, they should be given the opportunity to make acceptance of arbitration depend on certain conditions, in which case the tribunal would have to declare that the conditions would not obstruct its work. And the entire question should be fully clarified so that the opinion of the tribunal would be treated with respect, even if it was not able to provide a binding resolution.

By the use of sanctions on a basis of principles the tribunal may establish whether an existing agreement or compromise complies with principals as interpreted by the tribunal, whether it fits in with the concrete guiding principles and should be guaranteed by the great powers and the international institutions. While the task of giving an opinion is important in overcoming initial difficulties, the use of sanctions based on principles points towards further development. The situation today prescibes that a decision by experts or arbitrators and in accordance with basic principles should still take the form of a political agreement, a compromise between the powers, if it is to become valid; but in the long run political compromise should become valid when it has been sanctioned by an impartial agency by the authority of known principles.

It would be useful in international disputes for political arbitration to be linked to the international mediating function of the Security Council and the Secretary General, and to the delegating of mediators who are more politicians than arbitrators. In this case it would be important that the tribunal should first be able to establish the principles that would form the basis of settlement before or during a mission, and afterwards to be able to give its opinion on whether the compromise is in harmony with the formulated principle and whether it can be politically guaranteed.

Of course when necessary any decision could be divided into interim (based on principle) and final resolutions, possibly with a timetable for execution. The final decision must be guaranteed by the relevant political executive (security) councils of the regional organisation concerned or of the United Nations, and particularly by the major powers sitting in these councils, however the decision may have been effected – by its own resolution, by an international political body or by an international treaty. This would be more forceful than an ordinary international treaty in obliging the parties to honour the decision, not to amend it without the consent of the arbitrators and the guarantors and not to tolerate any propaganda against it.

Political side effects and additional obligations related to the tribunal's decisions

Political arbitration, precisely because it is political, may have desirable or undesirable side effects, and this is where the political judgement of the tribunal is most needed. It must keep the side effects in mind while retaining all the impartiality of the arbitration and the authority produced by this impartiality. At this stage it is not, of course, possible to lay down in detail how the tribunal may do this, but there are a few points that can be considered.

A significant feature of international political arbitration is that it takes place in an atmosphere of concessions, and one political side effect is promotion of this atmosphere, particularly for the party benefiting from the arbitration. In this respect it would be useful to establish an obligation for every country that has benefited from arbitration so that, in proportion to the benefit the country has received, it should allow possible disputed claims against itself to be submitted to arbitration. This could have a dual significance: it would help to loosen rigid attitudes, and it would increase the validity of the precept that a nation or state that is disinclined to recognise the validity of principles when used against itself should not be able to appeal to those principles in other cases. A reasonable sense of proportion needs to be observed, of course, in the interests of the psychological effects of the arbitration. But the political tribunal may, like the Secretary General of the United Nations, be able to use these factors intelligently so as to initiate political transactions for the benefit of world peace. These transactions might then be the modern democratic equivalents for the peacemaking of the territorial transactions of the former monarchs.

The effect upon the domestic political situation of the countries is another consideration. For each government concerned the tribunal's decision is seen as success or failure. And then there is the situation where, in the name of the principle of self-determination, a government benefits even though it does not itself respect the principle, and it governs in an oppressive manner. An example of this was the referendum in the Saar, which we have already mentioned, where the proper application of self-determination led to a government of gangsters gaining political advantage while the population brought tyranny upon itself through its right to self-determination being honoured. Yet impartial arbitration cannot let itself be influenced by the nature of the governments in the countries concerned, for it must have validity for the future that far transcends the life of any government. And the disastrous consequences of great powers taking a stand on the basis of their own immediate relationships with governments has already been mentioned — and is precisely why an impartial agency is needed.

The problem is not particularly difficult when a government is oblivious to elementary human rights, with its administration so insane that it is condemned by the majority of countries of varying political and social persuasions; and we have referred to the possibility of restricting the international rights of such countries, perhaps by this kind of impartial arbitration. It is easy to see that among the sanctions that could be taken against such governments, the application of the principle of self-determination in their favour should be suspended, by postponing either the passing of a resolution or the execution of a resolution.

But there are less extreme shortcomings to be found in the institutions of democracy and freedom, which may take the form of a coup or suspension of a constitution, and they cannot be ignored by the political tribunal when its driving forces are the principles of sovereignty of the people and self-determination. And the tribunal cannot remain blind to territorial changes that extend a country's authority, even when the changes have come about through legitimate means. The questions is to what extent the political tribunal can weigh up these considerations when an issue of state-formation or territorial alteration is submitted to it. Unless the shortcomings are the extreme ones mentioned, the tribunal cannot take formal notice of them, much less act upon them, as the tribunal is by no means an international constitutional court. The present structure of the international community precludes any interference with the domestic affairs of states except when the abuses are really flagrant ones, and if the tribunal attempted such interference it would risk losing the faith of countries and prejudice the gradual strengthening of its own powers and authority. And in applying its guiding principles, the tribunal cannot afford to show any displeasure with the domestic administration of a country, however serious its reasons for doing so, for then it would risk its status of impartiality, and might also be accused of passing long-term resolutions on the basis of short-term considerations.

There is no easy answer to this problem. One possibility might be to make it a condition of any arbitration that when a country acquires new territories as a result of international arbitration or gains recognition through arbitration, it must declare a comprehensive political amnesty covering both the country and the newly acquired territory. This would not be criticism or interference, but only humanitarian adjustment prescribing inner reconciliation prior to recognition of the new territory, and which would to some extent prevent political persecution or oppression in the new country or newly acquired territory. This is a proviso that could be applied to ideal democracies and backward military dictatorships alike; and other than something along these lines there is little that arbitration can do for this problem in normal cases.

The procedure for international political arbitration

It would be foolish at this time to try to specify in detail the procedure for international political arbitration, but there are some obvious indications which can be explored.

The tribunal as a kind of court is obviously limited by its terms of reference, and however widely it may interpret these terms it must not overreach the limits of its powers in its deliberations or in its actions. But it may declare that its powers are too narrow for it to be able to act in a case, and giving its reasons for this it can then offer views on some points of the case while suggesting the terms of reference that would allow it to approach the matter fully.

As a political tribunal, its procedure should be broader and more active than that of the ordinary international courts of justice. It must seek beyond the evidence of the litigants to discover all relevant facts; and it should limit the declarations of the litigants to a clarification of those facts that are essential for settlement. This means the careful definition and dissection of the whole problem and the detailed formulating of questions.

The tribunal may subdivide its decisions, distinguishing between preliminary and interim decisions, and decisions relating to the merits of the problem and affecting the execution of preliminary decisions; so it is possible for there to be a preliminary decision on principles as a framework for the tribunal's further work on a case. On this basis the parties will be asked to submit evidence and suggestions which the tribunal, using its own guiding principles, may refer to for a later decision. A preliminary decision may possibly require a referendum as a basis for a final decision; and even this may be divided into several questions that could involve more than one referendum.

The resolutions or decisions may cover a number of additional and executive problems, depending upon the extent of the tribunal's powers as much as the nature of the case in dispute. Examples of these might concern the matter of bases, neutral zones, minority rights, resettlements, objects of national value, the appointment of experts or specialist committees, interim precautions, guidelines for the execution of the final decision, the timetable, and so on.

Both the division and the merging of decisions have advantages, whether they be preliminary decisions of principle, final decisions, essential or procedural decisions. An advantage of division into part decisions is that it is then possible to clarify essential matters and principles in good time and thus help the direction of the debate; but because of the extra time this takes it might give opportunity and motive for the violent and one-sided creation of a *fait accompli*. And here is the advantage of compressing of decisions — the entire decision appears at once and with the full weight of finality. However, an attempt to make the decision fully comprehensive may also take time, during which there may be a change in the political balance that made arbitration possible in the first place. So the significance of the impartial arbitration together with the volatility of the political situation must determine how much division or merging of decisions there should be, and long experience in arbitration will be necessary for this.

Possible contents of decisions by the tribunal

So far as the possible content of the decisions or opinions of an international political tribunal is concerned, this would be governed by the problems of applying the basic principles of the international community as laid before the tribunal. It is worth repeating the concrete problems which may be brought to international arbitration. They are grouped according to subject matter.

1. *Questions related to applying the principle of self-determination in matters of state-formation and demarcation*

(a) When does the principle of self-determination entitle a people to form an independent state, and when does it entitle the population of a particular territory to transfer its allegiance from one state to another? How can it be judged whether it is a separate national entity that motivates a movement towards the formation of a sovereign state? How can the exceptional changes to national frontiers serve to strengthen international stability, with special regard again to the processes of nation-formation;

(b) How should the will of the population be given effect? When may the will of the people be presumed from undisputed facts or national allegiance, and when must the population be formally asked in a referendum? What are the criteria to be considered when popular will is to be presumed without plebiscite? More specifically, where and when must the demarcation line be drawn along historic borders, or along ethnic and linguistic borders, with perhaps other criteria to be considered? How should the questions in a plebiscite be put so that they are realistic, just and practical? Is it permissible to repeat a referendum, and if so in what circumstances? How is the result of a referendum to be interpreted if it should raise problems?

(c) If the will of the population is divided over territorial lines, which should prevail? And what should happen where territories contain a population that is a mixture of peoples with differing wills? What rights does self-determination give to minorities, or what rights can it give? That is, which territories can or must be considered indivisible as a unit, so that their fate must be decided by the majority of their population, and which territories can or must be divided on the lines of certain criteria or on the basis of a plebiscite? In other words, when must one apply the divided and expressed will of the population to the whole of the disputed territory, and when to the limited sectors of individual groups of people?

(d) When a population has changed its domicile, resettled, either voluntarily or under compulsion, what must happen then? What rights to self-determination does a population have when it has recently settled on a territory; When can the resettlement or exchange of populations be justified, and under what conditions?

2. Questions relating to the membership of states in the international legal community, their admission to it, and possible suspension of membership

(a) For the administration and government of a newly formed state, what are the requirements to be met in the spheres of public order, freedom, human rights, minority rights, etc., so that they conform to the commonly held requirements of the international community, but without regard to social and economic order?

(b) Again without regard to social and economic order, what are the generally dangerous and internationally irresponsible attitudes of principle, political systems and actions that justify suspension of membership rights in the international community, and within this membership of the United Nations and other specialist or regional organisations?

International political arbitration, as with any jurisdiction, must attempt to find individual solutions to these questions, solutions which meet the requirements of reality and principle equally. While related to principles, these solutions must concern the application or formulation of concrete and generally valid tenets resembling legal rules, which must be applicable for other cases as well within a certain sphere of validity. The general principles of the international community do not as yet have the concrete form that could be taken as legal rules, and so it is not possible to refer to existing rules or tenets; but these must be formed in the future in the context of actual cases. It is far too soon to draw up a system of desirable tenets, but it is possible to indicate them in the context of an analysis of some cases.

[12]

Conclusion and Summary

Our point of departure has been the paralysis and incapacity of the international community. We have contrasted the existing state of the international community with its precursor – the older, far less institutionalised yet far more workable system of the European monarchic community. We have searched for the reason why the latter was more successful in the consistent application of its governing principle, monarchic legitimacy, than the modern international community has been in applying its own governing principle: the self-determination of nations. We have seen why today almost every conceivable international procedure aimed at settling disputes, from war to action by the Security Council or plebiscites, is all but incapable of settling international disputes and of creating stable and legitimate order. One reason is the inadequate functioning of the institutions of great power agreement; and a second is the absence of agencies which could effect impartial international political arbitration. For it is a prerequisite for the working of any international procedure for settling disputes that the agreement of the great powers and their ability to take concerted action must be constantly and institutionally available.

The world organisations formed after the First and Second World Wars, however, have never become more than the forum of a potential, hardly as yet actual, international public opinion. And far from promoting concord between the great powers, which was the basic institution of the old European community, these new organisations nearly wrecked any chance at all of such a concord working. This concord ought now to find its expression in the working of the Security Council. Yet this body has become a second-rate international forum of inadequate efficacy, largely because no clear and valid processes have arisen; and there is no alternative and more efficient vehicle of power agreement. But if great power agreement could function successfully and evenly, then disputes could be settled – always given that some legitimacy or principles can be discovered when claims of state-formation or territorial demarcation are contested. Where such legitimacy for some reason either does not exist or is strongly questioned, great power agreement is no longer able to create new legitimacies so simply and naturally, nor to stabilise them so quickly, as did formerly the treaties of sovereigns who, in their persons, embodied monarchic legitimacy. Therefore the new, democratic and morally superior principle of self-determination requires a new and characteristic international agency. Such an exceptional yet permanent and institutional forum could apply impartially those basic governing principles of the international community which have not yet crystallised into international law. The most important of these is the application of self-determination in those periodic and inevitable disputes where new international legitimacies must be created.

Such an 'International Political Tribunal' would be the second remedy to the present incapacity of the international community; however, it is now extinct, at least in its institutionalised form, and it is no longer fashionable to use it even occasionally. Of course the two remedies can, in the last resort, be successful only when used together. Great power agreement and concerted action is successful only if it complies with the basic principles of the international community and can withstand the acid test of judgement by an impartial forum. This also means that the great powers, as a whole, must act more responsibly than other countries. On the other hand, any judgement or pronouncement by such an impartial forum, mandatory or otherwise, would be effective only if supported by the agencies of great power agreement and upheld by great power guarantees. These could provide the starting point for a real international integration. Short of these immediate steps, it is futile simply to look towards some desirable but remote state of affairs, e.g. the need for a world government, or world police force, no matter how justified these claims may be. But the form and manner of these two most pressing prerequisites of the structural development of the international community will vary in every actual case we might examine. International institutions will always need to be more flexible than national ones, but equally will develop their own working conventions as well as formal rules.

Certainly it is possible to argue against any hopes of strengthening the proper functioning of the Security Council and of the creation of an impartial agency for arbitration. If disputes involved basic conflicts, between the great powers, they could not be settled at all, or if lesser disputes, capable of agreement between the great powers, then they would be settled on that basis anyway. Our entire train of thought could be criticised as leaving unconsidered and unanalysed – for quite obvious reasons – those very political conflicts of the modern world which seem most impervious to solution: namely, the cases of divided countries in which the capitalist and the communist structures of society confront each other within one and the same nation, with the two opposing power blocs behind them. It would appear futile to speak of institutional forums, of the necessity of great power agreement, when the great powers are themselves in the forefront of the dispute. Nor would it seem that impartial forums could intervene since the opposing parties deny the possibility of impartiality in just such cases. The basic objection is that in these particular issues the problem is not of how to apply the principle of self-determination, but something quite different: irreconcilable social and ideological differences.

There is a lot of truth in all this, but basically these arguments are irrelevant to the essence of the matter. True, cases such as Israel/Palestine and Cyprus are ones where a final settlement could be made today, and not ones which at the moment are likely to prove incapable of conclusive solutions. But this is not to say that a better functioning of the institutions of great power agreement could not achieve some progress towards the solution of the problem of such divided countries, nor that agencies as impartial as today's situation would allow could not, with their pronouncements, contribute to solving these problems. Far less would it be true to say that the principle of self-determination, in the context of the international community, means no more than the application of democracy as a governing principle and as a basis for demarcation. In fact, the true problem of the divided countries is that, in them, the opposing regimes differ in their respective formulations of democracy and of the 'true' or 'full' meaning of self-determination. Accordingly, the international debates and struggles which surround these issues differ in one respect only from the more usual international political disputes: in these cases it is not the demarcation line between already existing or newly formed states that has to be settled, but the question of how a simple, democratic and 'legitimate' government can be established in a politically divided nation.

Ultimately, therefore, it is no less true of the problem of divided countries than of other issues that they can only be solved 'legitimately' through the valid application of these democratic principles which are, in fact, identical with the principles of self-determination. Here again, as in all other international disputes, the great object is to avoid unlawful violence. On the other hand, it is also true that, to solve the problem of the divided countries, neither the agreement of the great powers nor any kind of international political arbitration is enough. In such cases the slow but perceptible progress towards inner purification of the opposing political, social and ideological structures is also needed. Things would be easier if the great ideological powers in fact lived up to their own principles. But even at this point one can see the analogy with the classic international conflicts, for all experience shows that just as 'hot war' has ceased to be a procedure through which political disputes can be decided, so 'cold war' used for opposing ideologies is equally unsuited, without inner purification, to achieve a decision on the practical question of how democracy should be interpreted.

Despite all that has been written above about the correct interpretation of self-determination, it should be evident that the framework of a train of thought which aims at diagnosing the ills of the international community of states and finding remedies for them would be disrupted by any attempt to pass judgement on the internal democracy of the states concerned. This would have to be the subject of a different train of thought which, although having much in common with our present one, could hardly influence the main conclusion of this present study: that the two keys to the problems which now paralyse the international community are the improved functioning of the *already existing* agencies of great power agreement and the creation of new and exceptional institutions of impartial political arbitration. All we need to recognise is that this problem is but part of the larger question: why the greatest and most promising undertaking of modern mankind – the organisation of society on the twin bases of freedom and democracy – has, at several points, reached deadlock, and where the crucial ways to break out of this deadlock can be found? This is the question which we must all clearly and unequivocally try to answer, with respect both to the internal affairs of states and to the international community.

Index